THE DREAMING MIND

BUDDHISM'S WISDOM ON DREAMS AND THE NATURE OF REALITY

QUYEN NGO

THRESHOLD EDITIONS

Copyright © 2025 by Quyen Ngo

All rights reserved.

No part of this book may be reproduced in any form or by any electronic or mechanical means, including information storage and retrieval systems, without written permission from the author, except for the use of brief quotations in a book review.

"It is the mind that creates the world." – *The Buddha*[1]

CONTENTS

Preface	vii
AUTHOR'S NOTE	1
PROLOGUE — The Quiet That Rises Before Morning	3
CHAPTER ONE — The Creature That Dreams	7
CHAPTER TWO — The Dream That Began a World	14
CHAPTER THREE — Dreams in the Buddha's Early Life	26
CHAPTER FOUR — Dreams on the Eve of Renunciation	39
CHAPTER FIVE — The Five Great Dreams	44
CHAPTER SIX — The Night the Mind Opened	53
CHAPTER SEVEN — The Ending of the House	63
CHAPTER EIGHT — The World as It Is Seen	74
CHAPTER NINE — Nimitta, Visions, and the Shifting Texture of Consciousness	86
CHAPTER TEN — Dream Yoga Before Dream Yoga	97
CHAPTER ELEVEN — The Quiet Before the Last Journey	107
CHAPTER TWELVE — Dreaming in the Modern World	120
CONCLUSION: The Quiet Where Dream and Dawn Meet	127
A Note to the Reader	134
APPENDIX A: Dream Episodes in the Pāli Canon	135
APPENDIX B: Dream Symbolism in Early Buddhist Sources	139
APPENDIX C: Comparison of Dream Narratives in the Pāli Canon and the Lalitavistara Sūtra	143
APPENDIX D: How to Work with Dreams in Buddhist Practice	147

GLOSSARY OF BUDDHIST TERMS	153
Notes	159
Bibliography	165

PREFACE

This book began long before I wrote my first line of academic research. It began in childhood, on a night I still remember clearly—a night when I slipped into a dream and woke up inside it.

I did not know the term *lucid dream* at the time. I only knew that everything around me felt astonishingly real—more vivid, more textured, more alive than the world I returned to when morning came. I could see every shape sharply. I could feel the air. I could choose what happened next.

And when I finally woke, I lay still for a long time, unsettled by a quiet but persistent thought: *If a dream can feel this real, what exactly is "reality"*

It was the first time I sensed that the mind might not be as simple as it appears. That brief dream left a mark deep enough that I carried its question with me into adulthood.

Years later, when I began my Master's degree in Buddhist Studies, that question resurfaced with force. Dreams appeared everywhere in the early texts—in the Buddha's life, in the stories of monks and kings, and in teachings about mind, illusion, and awakening.

Preface

I wrote my thesis on dreams in early Buddhism. It was rigorous, structured, and grounded in academic method. Yet when it was complete, something still felt unfinished. The thesis answered scholarly questions, but it did not touch the sense of wonder that first drew me to the subject. It did not return to the mystery that had lingered since that childhood night.

This book is the version I always wanted to write.

It brings together the scholarship of that research, the poetic depth of Buddhist storytelling, and the universal human experience of dreaming. It is written for anyone who has ever woken from a dream and wondered what the mind is doing when the world dissolves. And it is written for readers who wish to encounter Buddhist dream teachings in a way that honors both accuracy and imagination.

Most of all, it is offered in the hope that dreams may be seen not as strange nighttime anomalies, but as windows into the nature of the mind itself.

Dreams changed the course of my life once. They continue to shape how I understand the world.

AUTHOR'S NOTE

This book presents Buddhist dream teachings through a blend of narrative, scholarship, and contemplative interpretation. Drawing from multiple genres of Buddhist literature—including early Pāli texts, commentarial sources, and later Sanskrit traditions—it moves between historical material and literary rendering with care.

All events, dreams, and teachings attributed to the Buddha or his contemporaries are grounded in recognized Buddhist sources. No dialogue has been invented for the Buddha, and nothing is placed in his mouth that cannot be traced to canonical or commentarial material. When scenes are written in a cinematic or poetic style, they are intended as literary renderings of documented traditions, not as fictional inventions.

At one point, the book introduces an interpretive hypothesis concerning prophetic dreams—specifically, the possibility that such dreams may arise when the mind senses karmic conditions approaching ripening. This proposal is not presented as doctrine or canonical authority. It is an inference drawn from early Buddhist teachings on karma, dependent origination, and the traditional classification of dreams, offered as a respectful contribution to ongoing discussion within Buddhist dream studies.

All other interpretations remain consistent with early Buddhist frameworks, even when expressed through modern language.

The aim of this book is not to romanticize dreams or to elevate them beyond their place in Buddhist thought, but to allow their subtlety to be felt. In the Buddhist tradition, dreams are one way the mind reveals itself. If the pages that follow help clarify that mind—in dreaming or in waking—then the purpose of this book has been fulfilled.

PROLOGUE — THE QUIET THAT RISES BEFORE MORNING

There is a moment before waking when the world has not yet decided what it is. Light has not fully gathered. Thought has not yet resumed its familiar weight. The self, that recognizable shape you step into each morning, is still loosening gently at the edges.

In this quiet interval, the mind drifts between what is seen and what is remembered, between what is imagined and what has not yet chosen a form.

Images rise without asking permission. A feeling lingers without explanation. A story presses forward before it has found a name.

For a brief, unguarded span, the ordinary rules of waking life feel negotiable.

Most people pass through this threshold without noticing. The alarm sounds. The body moves. The day asserts itself. Whatever hovered at the edge of awareness dissolves before it can be examined or held.

Yet even forgotten dreams leave traces. A heaviness carried quietly into the morning. A tenderness that opens without a clear cause. A question that follows like a shadow, long after its origin has faded.

These traces are not accidents. They are not decorative remnants of sleep. They are expressions of the mind in motion, revealing how experience forms, how meaning coheres, and how reality is quietly assembled before it is named.

It is here, in this unguarded crossing, that the mind reveals something it normally conceals, not through argument or analysis, but through direct experience.

This book begins at that threshold.

From the perspective of waking life, dreams are often treated as interruptions—odd, irrational events that vanish with the morning light.

They are dismissed as noise, as mental residue, as material best ignored in favor of what appears solid and useful.

Yet this dismissal is itself revealing. For in dreams, the mind performs openly what it does more discreetly during the day. It constructs a world. It assigns meaning. It generates emotion. And then it inhabits the world it has created as though it were unquestionably real.

In this sense, dreams do not differ in kind from waking experience. They differ in transparency. The processes that shape perception—memory, expectation, habit, desire—operate with fewer disguises. What is normally hidden beneath familiarity becomes visible.

Long before I encountered Buddhist texts, long before I studied how early traditions understood dreaming, I had a lucid dream I could not dismiss.

It was not remarkable because of its imagery, nor because it offered a message or symbol to interpret. It was remarkable because of the quality of awareness it carried.

Within the dream, there was a clarity that felt sharper than ordinary waking perception. Objects appeared vividly defined. Attention was stable. Experience unfolded with an immediacy that did not fracture into distraction.

When I woke, that clarity did not vanish.

I opened my eyes with a profound, almost alarming, sense that consciousness was wider, stranger, more luminous than the world I had been taught to trust.

I was young. Too young to understand that dreams sometimes reveal the mind as it is, rather than as we believe it to be. But something in me recognized what had occurred. That recognition never left.

For years, it remained unnamed, a quiet dissonance between what I experienced and what I was told about reality.

Dreams continued to arise, some ordinary, some unsettling, some charged with an intensity that exceeded their apparent content.

Only later, while studying Buddhist thought, did I encounter teachings that illuminated what had first appeared in that early dream. The Buddha's teachings repeatedly return to a simple but unsettling insight: experience is conditioned.

What we see, hear, think, and feel does not arise independently. It is shaped by habit, memory, intention, and attention. The mind does not merely receive the world. It participates in its construction. This insight lies at the heart of early Buddhist psychology. And dreams offer one of their clearest demonstrations.

In dreams, the mind constructs a world and then believes in the world it has constructed. Characters appear. Events unfold. Emotions arise with full intensity. Fear, longing, joy, and grief are experienced as real.

For the duration of the dream, there is no doubt.

And then the dream dissolves.

Its reality vanishes instantly, yet the feeling it carried may linger. The body remembers. The heart remembers. A mood, a question, or a subtle orientation travels forward into waking life.

Early Buddhism does not treat this as trivial. Nor does it treat it as supernatural. Dreams are understood as arising from causes—some physiological, some psychological, some shaped by habit and emotional residue, and some rare enough to alter the direction of a life. Throughout the Buddhist tradition, dreams appear at moments of transition and insight. A queen dreams of a white elephant before conceiving a future Buddha. A prince experiences unsettling visions that loosen his attachment to palace life. Practitioners encounter symbolic dreams as concentration deepens. Subtle, dreamlike perceptions arise as the body weakens and the structures of identity soften.

Dreams are not interruptions to the path. They accompany it. They reveal the mind's capacity to generate meaning, to construct worlds, and to believe in those worlds with absolute conviction.

This book approaches dreams neither as messages to be decoded nor as fantasies to be dismissed. It does not ask what dreams *mean* in a symbolic sense, but what they *demonstrate* about the nature of experience. How perception is shaped. How suffering arises. How the sense of self is constructed. And how insight begins when these processes are seen clearly.

For many readers, the most important spiritual questions do not begin in doctrine or philosophy. They begin in a personal moment—a dream, a vision, a disruption—that unsettles the certainty of the ordinary world. Such moments are not answers. They are openings.

The chapters that follow move between early Buddhist texts, historical accounts, and lived experience to explore how dreams illuminate the construction of reality and the possibility of awakening.

They ask a quiet but persistent question: if a dream can feel absolutely real and then dissolve instantly, what does this reveal about the reality we inhabit while awake?

For now, remain with the quiet just before morning—the fragile space where the mind begins to shape a world before the eyes have opened.

It is here, in this faint and private threshold, that understanding first takes root.

CHAPTER ONE — THE CREATURE THAT DREAMS

Night rested gently upon the ancient plain.

The fire had burned low, its embers glowing like small, breathing hearts beneath a thin blanket of ash. Beyond the circle of warmth, the land stretched wide and dark—a sweep of grass and scattered stone, accompanied by the quiet pulse of distant insects.

A lone figure slept beside the fire.

Their body lay close to the earth, shaped by it, as though the ground itself had made room. Breath moved slowly, deepening, softening, until the boundary between body and land seemed to loosen.

And then—the stillness shifted.

A finger twitched. The jaw tightened. The rhythm of breathing changed, as if answering something unseen.

A dream had risen.

Images formed without effort inside the quiet chambers of the mind: animals moving through tall grass, the echo of running feet, a river turning where it should not turn, glimmering beneath moonlight. A child's laughter. A shadow passing overhead. The sudden sensation of falling—and then, stillness again.

None of these images existed on the plain. Not one belonged to the night.

Yet to the dreamer, each arrived with the immediacy of life itself—vivid, complete, unquestioned.

The body stirred. A sound escaped the throat—half breath, half recognition—and the sleeper shifted, as though attempting to step into the world unfolding behind the eyelids.

The fire cracked softly.

The dream dissolved.

The figure woke.

At first there was only sensation: warmth fading from the skin, the pressure of earth against the back. Then breath settled. Awareness gathered. The gaze steadied beneath a sky crowded with stars, too many to take in at once. The moon hung low, casting pale light across the plain like a path not yet walked.

Something lingered, not the images themselves, which had already scattered, but the mood they carried: a residue of meaning without shape.

The dreamer sat upright and exhaled slowly, as though releasing something held too long.

This scene: simple, silent, ancient, is where the story of human dreaming begins.

Not with interpretation. Not with symbol. Not with doctrine or sacred text. But with a creature who slept and discovered, within that sleep, another world opening—a world made entirely of mind.

Long before language, before stories were shared around fires, before ritual or myth carried meaning across generations, the human mind was already dreaming.

Dreams arrived each night like the first art the mind ever created—shapes drawn without hands, voices heard without sound, movements felt without stepping. They were not recorded. No one named them. No explanation followed.

Yet they left traces. In breath quickened by fear. In hearts softened by relief. In small sounds that rose during sleep and drifted into the night.

Even at the very beginning, the mind was already exploring itself. It was already revealing its capacity to imagine—to construct worlds and dissolve them, to feel terror without danger, to feel joy without cause, to believe fully in what was not physically present.

Dreaming is older than language. Older than culture. Older than religion. It is one of the earliest ways a creature came to know that it possessed something like a mind.

Imagine the early human in the morning light after such a dream.

They rise slowly. They touch the earth with bare hands and feel cool air against the skin. Some dreams vanish instantly, leaving only a faint echo of emotion. Others remain—not as images, but as impressions that do not belong to waking life, yet feel too vivid to dismiss.

How would such a person understand this? The world they inhabit is solid: stone, soil, fire, wind. But the world they dreamed did not obey the same rules.

In dreams, rivers turn without bending. Animals appear without warning. Voices speak without bodies. Paths shift beneath the feet.

Here, without theory or explanation, the mind reveals its ability to generate reality and dissolve it again—independently of the physical world.

This observation is ancient. It did not begin with philosophy or psychology. It preceded both. From it would grow myth, story, and the earliest forms of spirituality.

Before humans prayed. Before they imagined gods or ancestors. Before belief took form. They dreamed.

Dreams were among the first teachers of mystery.

Modern science now describes dreaming in terms of neural processes: memory consolidation, emotional integration, pattern recognition. These descriptions are accurate. Yet they do not diminish the experience itself.

A dream feels real, completely real, until the moment it breaks. The mind believes in the world it creates until waking dissolves it instantly.

This simple, universal fact reveals something essential about consciousness: experience is not merely received. It is actively constructed.

We do not suffer because we dream. We suffer because we forget that waking life is also assembled moment by moment, through the same processes of interpretation, memory, and belief.

From this ancient ground, the chapter now widens.

Dreaming is not only a biological event. It is a window into the functioning of consciousness itself—a preview of how the mind imagines, interprets, responds, and creates meaning.

Here, long before Buddhism, before doctrine, before the Buddha's own dreams, we encounter the creature that dreams: a mind testing its own depths, a consciousness discovering its own landscapes, a human being touching worlds that exist nowhere but within. Dreams were among the first steps toward understanding mind.

The Dreaming Mind

In that ancient night beside the fire, the early dreamer unknowingly offered humanity its first glimpse of the world within the world, a glimpse that Buddhism would later illuminate with extraordinary clarity.

Thousands of years later, after humans shaped tools, stories, and ritual, a prince named Siddhārtha would turn his attention inward and examine the nature of experience with unprecedented precision.

He was not the first to dream. He was not the first to sense the fluidity of the mind. But he was the first to understand it completely.

Early Buddhism articulated what ancient dreamers had felt without language: that the world of dreaming and the world of waking are not opposites, but variations of the same mental processes; that experience is constructed moment by moment; and that suffering arises when what is constructed is mistaken for something solid. Dreams are not exceptions to this process. They are among its clearest demonstrations.

Return now, not to the ancient plain, but to your own experience.

Each night, you enter a world that feels real. You wake. That world collapses. Another takes its place. Two realities, each unquestioned while you inhabit them.

This is the mind's power. This is the mind's vulnerability. And this is the mind's beauty.

This is why dreams remain essential to Buddhist thought. They reveal the constructed nature of experience more gently, more intimately, than doctrine ever could.

This chapter marks the beginning of that recognition, a quiet return to the first truth the mind ever offered: you do not only live in the world outside you. You also live in the world within you. And the worlds you create, in dream and in waking, have far more in common than they appear.

ANALYSIS: THE CREATURE THAT DREAMS

This chapter establishes the methodological lens used throughout the book. Dreams are approached not as symbolic messages to be decoded nor as supernatural events requiring belief, but as lived experiences that make visible how the mind constructs reality.[1]

The opening vignette functions phenomenologically rather than historically. It illustrates what dreaming discloses before language, doctrine, or interpretation intervene: the mind's capacity to generate a coherent world, inhabit it fully, and dissolve it instantly. This capacity is not secondary to human experience; it is one of its earliest expressions.

From an early Buddhist perspective, this matters because Buddhist analysis begins with direct observation of experience rather than metaphysical speculation. Perception is not passively received; it arises through conditions—contact, feeling, recognition, and intention—unfolding moment by moment.[2] Dreams make this process unusually clear. When sensory input is reduced, the mind continues to fabricate experience using memory, emotion, and habit alone.[3]

For this reason, dreams are treated here not as exceptions to waking life but as concentrated examples of the same processes that shape ordinary experience. A dream feels real while the conditions supporting it remain intact. When those conditions change, the dream world collapses.

Early Buddhist analysis applies the same logic to waking experience: reality appears solid because its supporting conditions are usually unnoticed.[4]

This chapter also establishes a continuity between pre-theoretical human experience and later Buddhist articulation. Long before Buddhist texts described the constructed nature of experience, human beings were already encountering it nightly in their dreams. What Buddhism later clarified through disciplined investigation was not a new phenomenon, but a deeper understanding of a familiar one.[5]

Throughout the book, dream narratives from Buddhist sources are examined using this same approach. The analysis focuses on what dreams reveal about mental states, emotional momentum, karmic tendencies, and the shaping of perception. Some dreams arise from ordinary psychological causes; others reflect deeper conditioning; a small number are associated with moments of significant insight or transition. None requires supernatural explanation to be meaningful.

The purpose of analysis in this book is not to reduce dreams to theory nor to elevate them beyond experience, but to use them as windows into how the mind operates. Dreams show, in a compressed and intimate form, what Buddhist practice seeks to illuminate in waking life: the instability of constructed worlds, the ease with which they are believed, and the possibility of seeing through them.[6]

By beginning with the creature that dreams, the book grounds Buddhist dream analysis in a shared human experience, one that precedes culture, belief, and doctrine, and continues each night in the reader's own life.

CHAPTER TWO — THE DREAM THAT BEGAN A WORLD

Night in the Himalayan foothills had a softness that seemed to cradle the world. The mountains wore their darkness gently, the trees held their shadows close.

In a quiet chamber of Kapilavastu, under a canopy woven with gold thread, Queen Māyā slept.

A warm wind drifted through the latticework windows, stirring the jasmine vines outside. Moonlight pooled across the marble floor, and the faint rustle of peacocks settling in their roosts blended with the heartbeat of the night.

Her breathing slowed. Her hands relaxed on the silk coverlet.

And then, as though the world had been waiting for her to reach this depth of stillness, a dream approached.

Not a flickering image from memory. Not the restless replay of the day's impressions. But a dream so luminous, so complete, that it felt less like imagination and more like revelation.

∼

The Dreaming Mind

She stood on a vast plain, bathed in cool, moonlit clarity. The ground beneath her feet glowed faintly, as if lit from within. The air shimmered, alive, expectant, holding its breath.

Then, from the far edge of the plain, a figure appeared.

White. Radiant. Moving with a grace that seemed older than the world. A celestial elephant, pure as moonlight, with six tusks curved like crescents of polished ivory.[1] Its skin glowed with a gentle brilliance, not dazzling, but comforting, as though its presence itself was a blessing. In its trunk, it carried a lotus, pale as starlight.

Māyā felt no fear. Only a warmth, spreading through her body like the slow opening of a flower.

The elephant circled her once. Twice. A third time, each orbit releasing a wave of calm that washed over her mind, her limbs, her very breath.

Then, with infinite gentleness, it touched the lotus to her right side...

And entered her.

Not with force. Not with pain. But with a soft burst of light, beautiful, silent, complete.

She felt herself fill with something vast, pure, and utterly peaceful. A presence. A purpose. As if the dream were not merely a message, but a doorway.

The light faded. The plain dissolved. She woke.

Her hands rested naturally across her abdomen, as though cradling something already alive. Her heart felt clear. Her face glowed with a wonder she could not name.

At dawn, with the first blush of light on the palace roofs, she told King Suddhodana her dream.

The king listened in silence, his breath caught between hope and awe.

He summoned the court brahmins, their robes freshly pressed, their expressions solemn.

The queen retold the dream: the plain, the elephant, the lotus, the gentle entry through her right side.

The eldest brahmin bowed his head deeply.

"This dream," he said, "is not of the human world. It is the dream that appears when a Bodhisatta descends for the final birth. Your child will be a great ruler, or a Buddha."[2]

The chamber seemed to brighten. Suddhodana's pride swelled so suddenly he had to steady himself.

Queen Māyā touched her abdomen again, and felt, not movement, but a quiet warmth, as if her body remembered a light it could not yet describe.

The kingdom celebrated.

Something extraordinary had entered the human world.

Months passed, and the queen traveled to Lumbinī Garden when the time for birth approached.

The grove shimmered with blossoms, alive with bees, alive with spring.

Māyā reached for a sal branch, steadying herself, and gave birth standing, under the open sky.

The child emerged effortlessly, untouched by the impurities that accompany ordinary birth.

The early texts describe him not historically, but symbolically: the newborn stood upright, took seven deliberate steps, and lotus flowers bloomed beneath his feet. He gazed in every direction with fearless clarity and spoke words preserved in tradition:

"I am the foremost in the world."[3]

The Dreaming Mind

Attendants gasped. The king wept. Queen Māyā held her son with a joy so deep it trembled through her body.

The Bodhisatta had arrived.

And far beyond Kapilavastu, in mountains carved by wind and time, another story was beginning.

News of the birth spread like dawn, quiet at first, then brightening across the land. Merchants whispered of it in marketplaces. Farmers paused in their work, sensing something new in the air. Even the animals seemed strangely calm, as though the world itself was adjusting to the presence of a remarkable child.

But far from Kapilavastu, in the solitude of the Himalayas, the news arrived in a different way.

High in the mountains stood a hermitage of rough stone and wind-worn timber. There lived the sage Asita, called Kāḷadevala in some traditions, a recluse known for his discipline, his piercing clarity, and a serenity that made even wild animals approach without fear.

He spent his days in deep meditation, unmoving as a rooted tree.

On the morning of the Bodhisatta's birth, Asita emerged from his meditation to find the air strangely light, as if the mountain itself had exhaled a burden. He sensed joy. Not his own. But a joy that seemed to radiate from every direction.

He looked up. The sky shimmered with the presence of devas, moving in a graceful procession, their robes bright as lightning, their faces luminous with delight.[4]

Asita had lived a long life. He had seen omens, visions, rare celestial events. But never, not once, had he seen devas rejoicing openly in the human realm.

He raised his staff. "What has happened," he called, "that even the heavens celebrate?"

One deva paused mid-flight, bowing to the sage.

"A Bodhisatta has been born," the being said. "He will become a Buddha, a Perfectly Awakened One, unraveling the darkness that binds the world."

Asita's breath caught. All his life he had waited for this moment.

Without hesitation, he took his staff and began the long descent down the mountain.

The journey took days. He walked through forests alive with summer insects, across streams that sparkled in the afternoon sun, down slopes where the earth crumbled underfoot.

The world felt vibrant, not different in form, but different in meaning. Something had shifted.

When he reached Kapilavastu, the palace guards ushered him inside with reverence.

King Suddhodana greeted him warmly, for Asita was widely known as a sage of insight, a seer of rare integrity.

The king lifted his newborn son from the queen's arms and placed him gently into Asita's hands.

The sage expected to feel a child's warmth, a child's fragility. Instead, he felt stillness. A depth of stillness he had only ever touched in his deepest meditations.

The infant's face was calm, the eyes half-open, as though observing the sage from a place beyond infancy.

Asita examined the child's features, the long earlobes, the symmetrical limbs, the subtle marks that tradition preserved as signs of a great being.

Then the moment came.

Tears filled his eyes.

Not tears of sorrow, nor tears of joy, but something more intricate, a mixture of devotion, admiration, and grief.

He pressed his forehead to the child's tiny foot.

King Suddhodana stiffened.

"Sage," he said anxiously, "why do you weep? Is there misfortune in my son's future?"

Asita shook his head swiftly. "No, great king. This child will know no misfortune. He will become a Buddha, a teacher to gods and humans."

The king exhaled in relief. But Asita continued, his voice trembling: "I weep only because I am old. My life wanes. I will not live long enough to hear his teaching."

The room fell silent.

Queen Māyā held her breath.

Asita placed the child gently back into his mother's arms and bowed again, long and deeply.

"This birth," he whispered, "is the turning of an age." Then he rose, leaning heavily on his staff, and departed the palace—the last sage of the old world, walking away as the new world began.

Dreams as Portents: The Ancient Indian Understanding

In ancient India, dreams were not dismissed as idle flickering of the mind. They were thresholds, openings through which meaning, symbol, and karmic momentum revealed themselves.

People sought guidance in dreams before battles, rituals, and coronations. Mothers consulted dream readers when their children fell ill. Kings kept dream interpreters in their courts.

Dreams held weight. Dreams were respected. And among all dreams, those of conception were considered the most powerful.

Queen Māyā's dream was recorded, retold, memorized by generations.

It was not merely a symbolic story. It was considered the first act in the great movement toward awakening. For according to Buddhist tradition, the Bodhisatta's descent into his final birth occurs consciously, with intention, and with a clarity that surpasses ordinary minds.

The white elephant is a symbol of this purity. The lotus is a symbol of this undefiled nature. The right-side entry is a symbol that the birth will be free from defilement.

These images reveal not biology, but meaning. Not physical form, but spiritual pregnancy.

Māyā's dream marks the moment when awakening first touches the human realm. It is the opening of a cosmic story.

Asita's recognition is the second refrain, not symbol, but intuition.

Together, dream and vision link the inner and outer worlds, the psychological and cosmological. They show that truth begins in the mind, long before it appears in the world.

And the story of the Buddha begins not with renunciation, not with suffering, not with a quest, but with a dream.

The Meaning Beneath the Story

The stories of Māyā's dream and Asita's recognition are often read as myth, but in early Buddhist tradition, myth and meaning are not separate categories. These stories function on several levels at once.

On one level, they signal a rare birth, a being whose presence will alter the fabric of human understanding. On another, they reflect a sophisticated psychological insight: the recognition that the mind often knows truths long before the intellect knows how to name them. But perhaps more importantly, these stories illuminate a central theme of Buddhism: *the mind reveals truth through symbols when conceptual thought is not yet ready.*

For the majority of people, dreams are fragments, pieces of memory, fear, desire, habit. But for a mind in harmony with virtue, clarity, and karmic maturity, dreams can become refined instruments of insight.

Queen Māyā's dream is not accidental. It arises because the conditions for awakening have ripened across countless lifetimes. In this sense, the dream is the mind's echo of a deeper truth.

The white elephant does not come from outside her. It comes from within, from the subtle structures of karmic intention moving toward fruition. This is why the dream has such power: it is the meeting of the inner world and the cosmic purpose.

Asita's vision, though not a dream, continues the theme. His mind, sharpened by decades of contemplation, is open enough to perceive the world's shift. He does not imagine the devas' joy. He perceives it. His tears are not mystical exaggeration. They are the human response to recognizing greatness that he himself cannot witness fully.

In him, we see the poignancy of spiritual vision, not always dramatic, not always triumphant, but profoundly tender.

The Feminine and the Ascetic

This chapter also establishes a symbolic balance that will echo throughout the Buddha's life:

* Queen Māyā represents the *inner*, the receptive, the symbolic. She receives the Bodhisatta through a dream, a movement of the mind that bridges the human and the transcendent.

* Asita represents the *outer*, the ascetic, the intuitive insight born from renunciation.

One dreams. One sees.

One embodies creation. One acknowledges destiny.

These two forces, the fertile inner world and the disciplined outer path, must both exist for awakening to take root. And they are both part of every practitioner's path.

∼

Dreams as the First Teachings

Long before the Buddha teaches the Four Noble Truths, long before he speaks of craving, ignorance, or the constructed nature of perception, dreams speak first.

They reveal:

* the arrival of profound potential

* the shift in the world's moral landscape

* the readiness of a mind to awaken

These stories show that spiritual truth does not only emerge in meditation, scripture, or philosophical dialogue. It often begins in the mystery of the night, in the quiet places where symbols appear before language.

For modern readers, this is important. Dreams, too, can reveal our tendencies, our emotional truths, our fears, our longings. They can signal ripening karma, not as supernatural prophecy, but as the mind sensing what is already unfolding.

Māyā's dream and Asita's vision remind us that the mind is capable of extraordinary clarity when conditions align. They remind us that before awakening comes a whisper, a sign, a subtle shift in how the mind meets the world.

Before the Buddha awakens beneath the Bodhi tree, the story begins here: A luminous dream in the quiet chambers of Kapilavastu.

Two visions, one in sleep, one in meditation, opening the way for everything that follows.

The Dreaming Mind

The path to awakening does not begin with a struggle. It begins with a recognition. And recognition often begins in dreams.

~

ANALYSIS: DREAMS AS MIRRORS OF THE MIND

Early Buddhist tradition approaches dreams with a balance of respect and restraint. Dreams are neither dismissed as random neurological byproducts nor universally interpreted as supernatural messages from external realms. Instead, they are understood as expressions of mental conditions—revealing how perception, memory, emotion, and karmic momentum shape experience when sensory engagement is reduced.

Classical Buddhist sources describe dreams as arising from several distinct causes. Buddhaghosa, drawing on earlier tradition, outlines five primary categories: physical conditions of the body, residual impressions from past experience (*saññā*), ongoing mental preoccupations such as desire or anxiety, non-human influences under specific conditions, and, in rare cases, karmic processes approaching fruition.[5] Most dreams belong to the first three categories and reflect ordinary psychological functioning. Only a small number are regarded as significant indicators of future events.

Within this framework, Queen Māyā's dream is traditionally classified under the final category. Its importance does not lie in a literal interpretation of its imagery, but in what the dream signifies psychologically and ethically.

Early Buddhist tradition understands the dream as arising from a mind refined by virtue and karmic maturity, responding symbolically to conditions already in motion. The dream does not cause the Bodhisatta's birth; it reflects a convergence that has already occurred.

This perspective avoids both supernaturalism and reductionism. The white elephant, lotus, and right-side entry are not biological claims but symbolic representations of purity, clarity, and an undefiled birth. The dream illustrates an important Buddhist insight: under certain conditions, the mind can register karmic processes before they manifest outwardly. In this sense, the dream is not miraculous but rare—an expression of psychological coherence at an exceptional level of refinement.

Asita's recognition operates through a different mode of knowing. Unlike Māyā's experience, his insight does not arise through dreaming but through meditative clarity cultivated over decades. Early Buddhist texts distinguish such intuitive perception from imagination. Asita does not infer the devas' celebration; he perceives it directly, consistent with descriptions of heightened sensitivity available to accomplished ascetics.[6]

This distinction highlights an important aspect of early Buddhist epistemology: the tradition acknowledges multiple modes of cognition. Symbolic insight may arise through dreams, intuitive perception through meditative stillness, conceptual understanding through reasoning, and direct wisdom through awakening. Asita represents the highest form of insight available prior to the Buddha's teaching, and his tears express the poignancy of recognizing truth without being able to witness its full unfolding.

For contemporary readers, these narratives offer more than mythic biography. They point to a continuity of human experience that remains relevant. While modern individuals may not dream of celestial elephants, dreams continue to reveal unresolved emotion, latent desire, and emerging patterns that have not yet been integrated into conscious understanding. Dreams often register psychological and ethical movement before it becomes conceptually explicit.

This prepares the reader for one of Buddhism's central insights explored throughout the book: experience is actively constructed by the mind, moment by moment. Dreams make this process especially visible. In dreaming, entire worlds arise without external input, emotional tone shapes perception instantly, and the sense of self appears and dissolves with little resistance. The same processes operate in waking life, though they are usually obscured by sensory engagement.

Seen in this light, the dream of Queen Māyā and the vision of Asita are not exceptions to Buddhist psychology but refined demonstrations of it. Together, they introduce the book's central theme: *to understand dreams is to understand the mind, and to understand the mind is to take the first steps toward awakening.*

CHAPTER THREE — DREAMS IN THE BUDDHA'S EARLY LIFE

Night settled over Kapilavatthu with its familiar softness. Oil lamps glowed along the palace corridors. Attendants moved quietly, their footsteps hushed by woven mats.

Beyond the walls, the foothills of the Himalayas lay in cool shadow, their outlines barely visible against the winter sky.

In the inner chambers, a child slept. The infant prince who had been welcomed with omens and prophecies, with Queen Māyā's luminous dream and Asita's solemn blessing,[1] now lay curled on a soft cloth, his small chest rising and falling with a slow, steady rhythm.

The air around him held a gentle reverence, not the tense silence of fear, but the quiet of people who sensed something they could not name.

Some nights, the nurses would lean close and whisper that his sleep was "unusually light," as though he drifted very near the surface of waking. Other nights, they said he seemed "guarded", not by visible figures, but by a softness in the room, a calm that settled over anyone who stepped inside.

They did not speak of dreams directly. But they spoke of the way his face changed in sleep: how his brow sometimes furrowed as though he

The Dreaming Mind

were witnessing some distant sadness, how at other times his lips turned upward in a faint, untroubled smile, how he sometimes woke with clear, steady eyes and a gaze that seemed to look *through thing*s, not merely *at them.*

These details may not be historical. They are woven from later memories, commentary, and quiet devotion. But they point toward something true: from early childhood, Siddhārtha's inner life was unusually open. Not miraculous. Not theatrical. Just open. As though some part of him already sensed the fragility of human joy, the certainty of loss, and the possibility of a peace that did not depend on circumstance.

The palace was designed to protect him from everything unpleasant.

Servants smoothed every wrinkle from his path. Musicians played soft songs to drown out any sound of grief. The sick and the old were kept away from view.

The world he knew in those early years was carefully curated: only youth, only beauty, only vitality.

Yet even in this sheltered world, the mind did what minds always do: it dreamed. It shaped impressions. It built stories. It asked questions in the quiet where no one could hear.

Sometimes the child would grow still in the midst of play, his hand frozen in mid-air as though listening to something inward. Sometimes he would look up at his caretakers with a gaze too searching for his age. They would laugh softly, pat his head, and call him thoughtful. But what they were seeing was the early stirring of a mind that refused to be completely lulled to sleep.

There is a story that captures this with particular clarity: one year, when Siddhārtha was still very young, the royal family attended the ceremonial ploughing festival, a grand event marking the turning of the soil.

Men in fresh garments walked the boundaries of the field. Priests chanted. Offerings were made. Oxen strained at the ploughs, their muscles glistening in the sun.

Siddhārtha was placed beneath the shade of a rose-apple tree.

At first, the scene was filled with movement and sound: the scrape of metal against earth, the low calls of the farmers, the clink of ritual vessels. But the boy's attention settled on something else entirely. He watched as the blade of the plough cut through the soil. He saw worms and small creatures forced up into the light, their homes disturbed, their tiny bodies exposed to birds circling overhead. He saw the strain in the oxen's bodies, their breathing heavy, their skins marked by harness and rope. He saw the contrast between the festivity around him and the quiet suffering beneath it.

Something in him grew very still.

Later, the Buddha would recall this moment in the *Mahāsaccaka Sutta*, describing how, as a boy, he entered a natural, unforced stillness, a meditative absorption free from ill will, rooted in calm.[2] But at the time, no one knew what was happening. To the attendants, the child simply appeared unusually serene.

They found him sitting upright in the shade of the rose-apple tree, his body relaxed, his breathing slow. His face held an untroubled ease, a quiet joy that did not depend on any toy, any praise, any distraction.

They said he seemed to glow.

When they touched his shoulder and called his name, he looked up with a slightly distant gaze, as though returning from a space far wider than a child's nap.

They called it a kind of trance. But in the language of this book, we might call it a waking dream.

Not because it was unreal, but because his mind had briefly slipped out of the usual stream of palace conditioning and rested in its own natural clarity. A glimpse, perhaps, of the very mind that would one day sit beneath the Bodhi tree.

The Dreaming Mind

Queen Māyā did not live long after her son's birth. She passed away seven days later, leaving Siddhārtha in the care of her sister, Mahāpajāpatī.

But the echo of her dream did not vanish.

Dreams, especially clarity dreams, do not belong only to the dreamer. They shape the atmosphere around them.

Māyā's dream of the white elephant and the lotus was told and retold in the palace halls. It coloured how people looked at the child, how they spoke about him, how they understood his very presence. He was not treated as an ordinary heir. He was treated as one whose life would carry a meaning that could not yet be grasped.

This is part of the power of dreams: they do not only inform the person who dreams them. They inform the community that receives them. They become a lens through which events are interpreted. In this way, Māyā's dream quietly framed Siddhārtha's childhood.

Every moment of unusual stillness, every sign of gentle insight, every early expression of compassion was seen not as accident, but as confirmation.

Her dream had prepared the hearts around the boy to notice his depth.

As he grew older, Siddhārtha's dreams, if they were recorded at all, have not survived in detail. The Pāli Canon says almost nothing about the specific content of his childhood dreams. But Buddhist tradition remembers him as a child of unusual gentleness: easy to please, slow to anger, naturally inclined toward reflection.

The palace did everything it could to guard him from the rough edges of human life. Yet no wall is high enough to keep out dreams.

The body sleeps. The mind continues.

And in those quiet hours between dusk and dawn, when the palace lamps dimmed, and the corridors grew silent, it is not hard to imagine that Siddhārtha's mind wandered beyond the curated beauty around him.

Perhaps he dreamt of the fields and the workers he had seen from a distance. Perhaps he dreamt of the creatures unearthed by the plough. Perhaps he dreamt of ageing faces, sick bodies, or a grief he could not yet name. We do not know. But what we do know is that when, as a young man, he finally walked beyond the palace gates and saw an old person, a sick person, a corpse, and a renunciant, the sight did not just surprise him.

It pierced him.

It was not merely information. It was recognition. As though some quiet part of him had already turned these truths over in the dark. As though the seeds of renunciation had been ripening in him for a long time, in half-remembered impressions, in early intuitions, in dreams that left only a feeling behind.

In the life of every great teacher, we tend to focus on the dramatic moments: the night of departure, the long austerities, the final awakening. But long before these are subtler events: a mother's luminous dream, a sage's solemn recognition, a child's spontaneous stillness beneath a tree, a vague ache that comfort cannot soothe. These are the first movements of inner awakening. They rarely look like spiritual milestones. They look like small shifts: a child noticing suffering in the midst of celebration, a restless feeling that privilege cannot ease, a quiet joy that does not depend on what the world provides.

Dreams and dreamlike states are woven through these early years: Māyā's dream, the glow of Asita's intuition, the soft, contemplative space beneath the rose-apple tree. They are not interruptions of reality. They are preludes to it. They show that awakening does not begin with a grand decision. It begins with small moments of clarity that the world around us does not quite understand.

As you read this, you may recognize something of your own life in these early scenes.

Perhaps you, too, had dreams as a child that felt larger than your life. Perhaps you sensed, even when young, that the roles handed to you did not quite fit. Perhaps you felt a quiet, wordless question beneath all the things you were told to want.

Buddhism would not dismiss this as imagination. It would call it a kind of early knowing. A sense that the life you are expected to live is not the whole story.

In Siddhārtha's case, this early sensitivity would one day become the force that carried him out of the palace.

In your case, it may be the force that carries you inward, toward a more honest conversation with your own mind.

Clarity often begins not with certainty, but with a faint unease, not with a vow, but with a question, not with a grand dream, but with the sense that something in you cannot be fully satisfied by what everyone else seems to accept. These are not problems to fix. They are invitations. Invitations to see with a deeper eye, to listen with a quieter mind, and to notice the dreams, nighttime and waking, that keep pointing you toward a different way of being.

In the Buddha's life, the early years were not a waiting room before the path began. They were part of the path. The subtle dreams, the early intuitions, the gentle but persistent sense that something was off, these were the first cracks in the palace walls.

And in your life, the small, recurring dreams and quiet insights that refuse to go away may be serving the same role. Something in you may already be turning toward awakening, slowly, softly, without fanfare, just as it did for a child sitting beneath a rose-apple tree.

ANALYSIS: DREAMS, EMOTIONAL MEMORY, AND THE CONTINUITY OF MIND ACROSS LIFETIMES

This chapter sits at an important hinge in the book.

We are no longer in the purely mythic space of Queen Māyā's dream or Asita's recognition. We are now inside the slow, quiet shaping of a child's mind.

What we see here is not yet awakening, not yet renunciation, not yet the great turning, but the early movements of a consciousness already prepared for something vast.

What Surfaces When the Mind Is Quiet

Early Buddhism never lays out a modern theory of the "subconscious," but its psychology is clear:

* The mind holds *latent tendencies* (*anusaya*)

* *Habits and impressions* (*saṅkhāra*) continue beneath awareness

* Past experiences, actions, and intentions leave traces that later surface as thoughts, impulses, and dreams

When a child sleeps, or enters a quiet, absorbed state, these deeper layers have room to appear. They do not appear as doctrine. They appear as:

* moods

* images

* wordless intuitions

* strange familiarity or unease

In this way, dreams and dreamlike states are not random illusions. They are places where the mind's deeper movements become visible.

The Dreaming Mind

This chapter suggests, carefully, without over-claiming, that Siddhārtha's early experiences reflect just such surfacing:

* a softness toward suffering when he watches the plough disturb the soil

* a natural ease with stillness beneath the rose-apple tree

* a quiet discontent within a palace designed to satisfy every desire

These are not yet enlightenment. They are *preparations*.

Not because "awakening is remembering," but because the final awakening of a Buddha rests on a long, patient ripening of countless previous lives.

The Rose-Apple Tree and Spontaneous *Jhāna*

The most striking detail, anchored directly in the Canon, is the boy sitting under the rose-apple tree.

In MN 36 (*Mahāsaccaka Sutta*), the Buddha later recalls:

"Quite secluded from sensual pleasures, secluded from unwholesome states, I entered and dwelt in the first jhāna..."[3]

He remembers this as a child's natural, unforced experience of deep meditative absorption.

Much later, during his austerities as an adult, he will recall that moment and realize:

"That pleasure has nothing to do with sensuality or unwholesome states. That is the path to awakening."[4]

This does **not** mean he was already awakened as a child. It means that, as a boy, his mind touched a state that would later become a key to liberation.

Here is the crucial point: the jhānas are not easy. DN 2 (*Samaññaphala*

Sutta) describes them as the refined fruition of ethical training, sense restraint, and collected effort.[5]

Yet the child Siddhārtha slides into this state spontaneously.

From an early Buddhist perspective, this is not an accident. It is a karmic echo.

The Jātaka literature—stories the Buddha uses to teach—depicts him across many lifetimes as:[6]

* hermits in the forest

* skilled meditators

* sages devoted to renunciation

* practitioners of loving-kindness and wisdom

Whether or not one takes each story literally, they all make the same doctrinal point: qualities like deep concentration and compassion are not born in a single life. They are accumulated over many lifetimes.

So when the boy under the rose-apple tree slips into jhāna without training or instruction, it fits the logic of the tradition:

* the mind has been here before

* the capacity has been cultivated

* past cultivation appears now as ease in stillness.

This is not awakening. It is readiness.

The Buddha's enlightenment at Bodh Gaya is the culmination of his fully ripened *pāramī over countless lives* but childhood moments like this are traces of that long preparation quietly shining through.

Dreams, Quiet States, and the Mind Beneath the Surface

Although the Canon does not record Siddhārtha's childhood dreams, this chapter stays close to what we know about how the mind behaves.

When the palace sleeps and the corridors grow still, the body rests but the mind continues.

Early Buddhism and later Abhidhamma analysis both suggest that:

* the stream of consciousness never fully stops in life

* latent impressions can arise when external input is low

* dreams reflect these inner conditions in symbolic or indirect ways.

In that light, it is natural to imagine that the boy who:

* feels unease beneath curated luxury

* is moved by tiny creatures overturned by the plough

* rests easily in non-sensual joy would also have a rich inner life at night.

We do not know what his dreams contained. What we can say, in line with the tradition, is this: when the mind grows quiet, deeper tendencies surface. In sleep, in meditation, and in moments of stillness, the movements that usually remain hidden become more visible—sometimes as dreams, sometimes as a subtle clarity. Buddhist commentary later gives shape to this insight by treating dreams as conditioned events, arising from the same factors that shape waking experience. Seen in this light, Siddhārtha's early stillness, his sensitivity to suffering, and his natural ease in meditative absorption appear not as isolated marvels, but as early expressions of a mind already inclined toward calm and clarity.

∽

Conditioning, Roles, and the Inherited Dream of Identity

This chapter also shows how early conditioning and deep karmic tendencies interact.

From one side, the palace projects a powerful dream:

* you are a prince

* you will be a world-ruler

* pleasure can protect you from pain

* beauty can hide suffering

* this is what a successful life looks like

From another side, his deeper tendencies do not fully accept this. His mind:

* grows still where others are excited

* feels compassion where others see only ceremony

* senses unease where others see comfort

This is where dreams, in the broad sense of the word, become important. We tend to think of dreams as only what happens at night. But early Buddhism also invites us to see that:

* cultural roles

* family expectations

* social ideals

are **waking dreams**, shared constructions that shape how we see ourselves.

Siddhārtha's early life shows a gentle but persistent friction between those outer dreams and his inner knowing. He is not yet awakened. But something in him refuses to sleep completely inside the role designed for him. That refusal is one of the earliest marks of a Buddha-to-be.

Why This Matters for a Modern Reader

For someone reading this today, the details of palace life and ancient festivals may feel far away. But the underlying pattern is close. Many people can recall childhood moments of:

* sudden compassion

* unexplained sadness

* a sense that others were ignoring something important

* a feeling that the life on offer was not the whole story

* dreams so vivid they stayed with them for years

Early Buddhism would not dismiss these as fantasy. It would see them as signs that deeper currents are already moving:

* subconscious processing of what has been seen and felt

* latent karma beginning to ripen

* quiet intuition that the "normal" world is incomplete

In Siddhārtha's story, these early movements foreshadow his later path.

In your life, they may be pointing toward your own work:

* to notice the "waking dreams" you inherited from family and culture

* to pay attention to the images and feelings that surface in sleep

* to trust that the mind, when quiet, often shows you what you most need to see

Not because you are already awakened—but because the conditions for deeper understanding are already moving within you.

∼

From Subconscious Surfacing to Conscious Path

The key insight of this chapter is subtle: *awakening does not begin with the moment of enlightenment.*

For a Buddha, that moment is unique, final, irreversible. But the conditions that make that awakening possible begin long before:

* in past lives of cultivation

* in early glimpses of clarity

* in childhood impressions

* in subconscious surfacing through dreams and stillness

The child under the rose-apple tree is not yet the Buddha. But the mind that will one day awaken is already showing itself. And in a quieter, humbler way, the same is true for anyone who has ever felt:

* a dream that will not let go

* a question that will not be silenced

* a tenderness that does not fit the world's hardness

These, too, are early movements of the path. Not enlightenment, but the subtle currents that make genuine practice possible.

CHAPTER FOUR — DREAMS ON THE EVE OF RENUNCIATION

Night settled over Kapilavatthu with an unfamiliar weight. The palace corridors, usually alive with soft music and murmured voices, had fallen silent. Oil lamps burned low, their flames wavering as though the air itself were uneasy.

Beyond the walls, the foothills of the Himalayas rested in shadow, their outlines faint beneath the winter sky.

Inside the inner chambers, Yaśodharā woke suddenly. Her breath caught. Her heart raced, a sharp, metallic fear pressing against her ribs.

She sat upright in the darkness, one hand clutching the coverlet, the other pressed to her chest.

The dreams—not one, but many—still clung to her like damp cloth. She closed her eyes, but the images returned.

∼

In one dream, the full moon fell from the sky. Not gently. Not slowly. It tore loose, plummeting toward the earth, shattering on impact into fragments of pale silver. The night went dark.

In another dream, her hair—long, heavy, carefully adorned—fell from her head in thick coils, scattering across the floor of her own chamber. She reached for it. Her hands closed on emptiness.

Then came the sound of breaking. Bracelets snapped. Earrings split. Necklaces shattered. Every ornament she had worn since girlhood fell away at once, as though the future itself had fractured.

In another dream, a mountain she had always known as immovable crumbled before her eyes, stone dissolving into dust.

And finally, the dream that pierced deepest, she saw Siddhārtha walking away, toward a dark forest. His steps were steady. His back turned. He did not look back.[1]

∽

She reached for him. "Siddhārtha," she whispered, her voice trembling.

He woke at once, as he always did—quietly, without confusion, his eyes clear as though emerging from deep water.

When he saw her shaking, he turned fully toward her.

"I dreamed," she said. "They were terrible dreams."

He listened as she spoke of the falling moon, the broken ornaments, the crumbling mountain, the hair scattered on the floor, and finally the image of him walking alone into the forest.

The room seemed to tighten around them, as though the night itself were listening. When she finished, her voice fell to a whisper.

"I feel," she said, "as if something is being taken from me."

Siddhārtha did not deny what she had seen. The symbols were clear. But truth, offered without care, can wound. He took her hands into his. "Dreams," he said gently, "often arise from the heart's fears. They show change in exaggerated forms."

"The moon?" she asked.

"Even the moon must wane," he said softly, "before it grows full again."

"And the ornaments?"

"They may be burdens loosening."

"And the mountain?"

"Even mountains do not remain unchanged."

She hesitated. "And the last dream? The one where you walked away?"

He paused.

A long pause.

"Sometimes," he said at last, "the mind imagines separation when the heart fears losing what it loves." He touched the tears on her cheek. "I am here now."

It was not a lie. But it was not the whole truth.

Yaśodharā's breathing slowed. Eventually, sleep returned—lighter, uneasy.

Siddhārtha remained awake. He turned his gaze to the small figure sleeping beside her. Rāhula lay curled, one hand near his cheek, his face untroubled. Siddhārtha felt his heart tighten. This was the cost.

When the moon reached its highest point, he rose.

The corridors lay empty.

Guards slept more deeply than usual. Lamps flickered, casting long shadows across carved pillars and polished stone.

He passed the training yard.

The council hall.

The inner gardens where he and Yaśodharā had once walked together.

Each place held memory.

Each memory asked him to stay.

But beneath the tenderness was clarity—unavoidable, unyielding.

When he reached the outer gate, Channa waited with Kaṇṭhaka.

No voices spoke. No signs appeared. Only breath, hoof, and heart.

The Great Departure had begun.²

ANALYSIS — DREAMS, ATTACHMENT, AND THE THRESHOLD OF RENUNCIATION

The dreams attributed to Yaśodharā do not appear in the early Pāli Canon. They emerge in later biographical traditions, most notably the *Lalitavistara Sūtra*, where they function as symbolic expressions rather than historical reportage.³

This distinction matters.

Buddhism does not treat dreams as external messages imposed upon the mind. They arise from conditions already present—attachment, intuition, emotional attunement, and the mind's sensitivity to impermanence.

Yaśodharā's dreams do not predict the future.

They *recognize* it.

Each image speaks the language of loss:

* the falling moon—the loss of a guiding presence

* the breaking ornaments—the collapse of worldly security

* the crumbling mountain—the end of what seemed unshakable

* the loosening hair—the stripping of identity

* the solitary figure—separation without return

Dreams surface where speech fails. They reveal emotional truth before the intellect can bear it.

This is why Siddhārtha's response is so restrained. He does not deny the dreams, but he does not confirm their sharpest meaning either.

In Buddhist ethics, truth must be spoken in ways that reduce suffering, not increase it.

The dreams do not *cause* renunciation. They reveal its *human cost*.

Siddhārtha's path has been forming long before this night—across years of reflection and, according to Buddhist doctrine, countless previous lives dedicated to fulfilling the pāramitās.[4] His departure is not escape, nor rejection, but necessity.

For Yaśodharā, the dreams mark the beginning of grief. For Siddhārtha, they mark the moment when compassion can no longer remain enclosed.

Dreams often arise at thresholds—moments when a life can no longer continue unchanged. They do not command. They illuminate.

In this way, Chapter Four shows that awakening does not begin in certainty or triumph, but in tenderness—where love meets impermanence, and the heart learns that letting go is not abandonment, but the first movement toward freedom.

CHAPTER FIVE — THE FIVE GREAT DREAMS

The night before awakening did not announce itself.

There was no thunder, no omen streaking the sky, no voice whispering from the dark. Only the quiet breathing of the river.

Siddhārtha lay beneath a sparse grove near the banks of the Nerañjarā, the ground cool beneath his thin mat, the stars steady and indifferent above him. He had walked a long road to arrive here.

Years of wandering. Years of striving. Years of pushing the body to its furthest edge, until even hunger lost its drama and pain became a familiar companion. He had learned what effort could do. And what it could not.

That night, his body was tired but not depleted. His mind was alert but no longer searching wildly. Something had gathered. Not triumph. Not certainty. A readiness. As though the mind itself had drawn inward, quietly arranging its final movements.

Sleep came gently. And in that sleep, the mind did not scatter. It clarified.

The Dreaming Mind

What arose were not ordinary dreams born of memory or fatigue, but visions the Buddha would later recount as the *Five Great Dreams*—dreams that appeared when the mind stood at the threshold of awakening.[1]

They unfolded one by one, without haste.

The First Dream

He lay down. But the ground beneath him was not earth as he had known it. It was the entire world. The great mass of land curved beneath his body, rivers threading through valleys, plains stretching without end, mountain ranges rising like ancient ribs. His head rested upon the Himalayas, cool and immovable. One hand reached to the eastern sea. The other touched the western ocean. His feet extended toward the southern waters.[2]

He did not feel vast.

He felt *placed*. As though the whole of existence had become the field upon which his life would unfold.

The dream held him there, not as a ruler, not as a conqueror, but as a being whose concern had grown wider than self.

Then the image loosened and slipped away.

The Second Dream

From the center of his body, at the navel, a gentle brightness appeared. From that brightness, a vine emerged. Slender. Living. Unforced. It rose steadily upward, passing beyond the trees, beyond the clouds, beyond the visible sky, until it reached the realm of the gods. Then it branched. One tendril reached east, another west, another north, and another south. Each branch extended without strain, as though growth itself were the vine's only nature.

Siddhārtha watched without grasping, without fear.

The dream did not say *what* would grow. Only that something would.

And that it would not belong to him alone.

∽

The Third Dream

He stood upon pale ground. From the earth at his feet, white worms began to rise. They covered his soles, his ankles, his calves, gathering quietly, persistently, without harm.[1]

There was no disgust. No revulsion. Only the unmistakable sense of being surrounded. Of becoming a center to which many small lives were drawn.

The worms did not bite. They did not wound. They simply gathered, patient, numerous, inescapable. And Siddhārtha understood, without needing words:

To be awakened is also to be approached.

The dream dissolved.

∽

The Fourth Dream

Birds filled the sky. They came from every direction, near and far, high and low. Birds of many colours: dark, bright, mottled, pale. They wheeled above him, a living pattern of difference. Then, one by one, they descended. And as they drew near, each bird turned white.[1] Not blinding white. Not ornamental. The white of cloth washed clean. The white of simplicity.

They gathered at his feet, wings folded, voices silent. The air grew still. The difference remained, but the hostility did not.

The dream rested in that stillness for a long, quiet moment before fading.

∽

The Fifth Dream

The final dream rose without drama. No sky split open. No light descended.

He stood. Beneath his feet was a vast mound, a mountain of refuse, dark and steaming, layered with the waste of countless lives. The stench should have been overwhelming.

It was not.

The filth should have clung to his body, marked his skin, soiled his robes.

It did not.

He stood upon it untouched.

The mass beneath him did not collapse, did not swallow him, did not stain him. It simply *was*, heavy, unavoidable, the accumulation of the world's discards.

Birth and decay. Desire and aversion. Greed, hatred, delusion. The uncountable by-products of conditioned life.

And yet, he remained clean.

Not lifted above it.

Not separated from it.

Standing fully upon it, yet unsoiled.

The dream held this image for a long, silent moment. Then it released him.

ANALYSIS: THE FIVE GREAT DREAMS AND THE PSYCHOLOGY OF PRE-AWAKENING

The Pāli Canon records the so-called *Five Great Dreams* as occurring on the night immediately preceding Siddhārtha's awakening. Their presentation is notably restrained. They are not embedded in dramatic narrative, nor are they interpreted as supernatural communications from external agents. Instead, they appear as matter-of-fact indicators that something decisive has already taken shape within the mind.

This restraint is significant.

Early Buddhism does not treat dreams as prophecy in the common sense. Rather, it understands them as *expressions of mental conditions*. When the mind is burdened by craving, aversion, and confusion, dreams tend to be disordered. When the mind has been purified through sustained ethical discipline, concentration, and wisdom accumulated over long practice, dream imagery becomes coherent, symbolic, and revealing.

The Five Great Dreams should be read in this light: not as predictions of future events, but as diagnostic signs of a mind that has reached a point of irreversible maturation.

Dream One — The Measure of Capacity

In the first dream, Siddhārtha lies upon the earth itself, with the Himalayas as a pillow and the oceans touching his limbs. The imagery does not suggest conquest or domination. He does not stand above the world; he rests upon it.

This distinction aligns closely with early Buddhist understandings of awakening. Liberation is not portrayed as withdrawal from the world, nor as mastery over it, but as the capacity to remain fully present without being overwhelmed. The dream reveals a mind capable of encompassing the totality of experience—pleasant, painful, and neutral—without grasping or resistance.

From a doctrinal perspective, this reflects the stabilization of *upekkhā* (equanimity), not as indifference, but as balanced awareness. The dream signals that the scope of Siddhārtha's compassion and insight has expanded beyond the limits of self-reference.

Dream Two — Teaching as Consequence, Not Intention

The second dream describes a vine rising from Siddhārtha's navel and spreading outward in all directions. The image is organic and unforced. The vine grows because growth is its nature, not because it is commanded to do so.

This resonates with the early Buddhist conception of Dhamma transmission. The Buddha does not "create" a teaching in the conventional sense. Rather, teaching emerges naturally as a consequence of realization. The vine does not represent ambition or deliberate expansion; it represents inevitability.

The origin of the vine at the navel—the bodily center associated with vitality and balance—underscores a key Buddhist principle: insight is embodied. Wisdom does not arise from abstraction alone, but from the integration of body, mind, and ethical conduct.

Dream Three — Discipleship Without Defilement

The third dream, in which white worms gather around Siddhārtha's legs without soiling him, is often misunderstood if read through a purely symbolic or moralizing lens. In the canonical and commentarial traditions, the worms represent disciples—numerous, persistent, and varied.

The dream does not deny the social consequences of awakening. It acknowledges that realization attracts attention, devotion, and reliance. What the dream clarifies is that such proximity need not entail corruption or attachment.

From a psychological standpoint, this reflects the maturation of non-clinging (*anupādāna*). Presence among others does not imply identification with them. Responsibility does not require possession.

Dream Four — Liberation Beyond Social Distinction

In the fourth dream, birds of many colors approach Siddhārtha and turn white upon arrival. In the social context of ancient India, color carried strong connotations of caste, status, and inherited identity.

The dream does not erase difference; it dissolves hierarchy. Whiteness here signifies simplicity, ethical purity, and renunciant orientation—not homogeneity. The image anticipates a community formed around practice rather than birth, a principle that would later challenge entrenched social structures without direct polemic.

This dream reflects a core Buddhist insight: suffering is universal, and so is the capacity for liberation.

Dream Five — Remaining in the World Without Being Claimed by It

The final dream, in which Siddhārtha stands upon a mountain of dung without being defiled, is among the most psychologically revealing. In early Buddhist symbolism, dung often represents what the world produces in abundance: wealth, praise, blame, offerings, status, and distraction.

The dream does not depict escape from these conditions, but immunity to them. The awakened one does not stand outside society; he stands within it without being absorbed.

This is consistent with the Buddhist understanding of renunciation as an inner transformation rather than a spatial one. Freedom is defined not by absence of contact, but by absence of attachment.

Author's Hypothesis — Karmic Ripening and Dream-Intuition

(The following interpretation represents the author's analytical contribution and is not stated explicitly in the early canonical texts.)

The Five Great Dreams can be understood as *manifestations of karmic ripening* operating at the level of subconscious intuition. According to Buddhist doctrine, the Buddha did not arrive at awakening through a single lifetime of effort, but through the fulfillment of the *pāramitās* across innumerable lives, as attested in the Jātaka tradition.

From this perspective, these dreams do not introduce new information. They articulate, in symbolic form, a realization that has already matured beyond conceptual thought. The subconscious mind, unencumbered by discursive reasoning, becomes the medium through which this accumulated karmic momentum briefly surfaces.

This suggests a model of dream-intuition in which the mind, when sufficiently purified, can apprehend—not by inference, but by direct sensitivity—the direction in which its own conditions are already moving. Dreams at this level are not random; in the commentarial sense, *the dream functions as a portent*—not as superstition, but as a sign that coherence has formed between past cultivation, present clarity, and what is now nearing ripeness. In this sense, the dream does not initiate awakening so much as confirm that the conditions for Buddhahood have gathered to completion.

The Five Great Dreams occupy a unique position in the Buddha's life narrative. They arise after years of disciplined striving and immediately before the final breakthrough. Their calm symbolism, doctrinal coherence, and psychological depth suggest a mind no longer searching, but settling.

They remind us that awakening is not sudden in its preparation, even if it is decisive in its moment. Long before insight becomes explicit, it reorganizes the mind from within.

And sometimes, the mind reveals that reorganization most clearly when it is no longer awake.

CHAPTER SIX — THE NIGHT THE MIND OPENED

Night descended over Uruvelā with the soft, steady weight of something ancient, not pressing, not threatening, only present.

The Nerañjarā River moved nearby, unseen in the darkness, its current whispering through reeds like a long breath exhaling.

Above, the branches of the great fig tree held the sky in fragments, stars caught between leaves, shivering points of light in a still, watchful blue-black.

Siddhārtha sat beneath it as if he had always been meant to sit here. His body carried the history of years: the long wandering, the teachers whose answers had not reached deep enough, the austerities that had sharpened his resolve while hollowing his flesh.

He had known extremes.

He had tasted their emptiness.

And now, having stepped back from self-torment, having steadied the body with food and the mind with balance, he had come to the edge of something he could feel but not yet name.[1]

The earth beneath him was cool. His spine rose gently, as if the body remembered how to be a mountain without effort. His hands rested one in the other, quiet as folded wings. Around him the world continued, insects turning their small lives over in the dark, the river doing what rivers do, the tree holding its patient silence.

And within him, the mind began to settle.

Not by force.

Not by command.

It settled the way muddy water clears when no hand stirs it.

Thoughts still rose, a flicker of memory, a fragment of fear, a trace of longing, but they rose lighter now, as if the mind no longer believed it had to follow them.

Breath after breath, the mind grew steadier.

The night deepened.

And in that deepening, concentration gathered, not as tightness, but as a single, unwavering clarity.

As the discourses describe, the mind entered the stillness of absorption, the quiet refinement that leads beyond pleasure and pain into a purity of equanimity.[2]

Nothing dramatic happened.

No thunder split the sky.

No voice announced a threshold.

Only this: The mind became bright, clear, pliant, steady, as if it had been waiting its whole life to become itself.[3]

The First Watch: Memory Without Beginning

When the mind was thus collected, it turned, not outward, but inward, toward a depth that ordinary attention cannot touch. And there, memory opened.

Not the small memory of childhood alone, not the near memory of the palace, but memory stretching backward as though time were not a line but a vast field.

Lives appeared.

Not as stories to entertain him, but as experience, one after another, forms arising, dissolving, arising again.

Names.

Places.

Conditions.

Joy.

Grief.

Attachment.

Loss.

A thousand ways of trying to be safe.

A thousand ways of trying to be loved.

A thousand ways of trying to outrun what cannot be outrun.[4]

In that seeing, the pattern became unmistakable:

The cycle was not cruel by accident.

It was lawful.

It continued because its causes continued.

And beneath the sheer expanse of it, a tenderness rose, not sentimental, not fragile, but vast.

A compassion large enough to include every self he had been, every being caught as he was caught, every life moving through the same repeating weather of wanting and losing.

The First Watch completed itself in silence.

The Second Watch: The Law That Cannot Be Bargained With

The night moved on.

The stars did not change their song, but something in the mind sharpened further, as if the lens through which reality is seen had been cleaned down to the last smear.

Then the second knowledge arose: the seeing of beings passing on according to their actions, not by divine preference, not by punishment, not by blessing, but by the quiet mathematics of cause and effect.

Lives moved like lights in a dark vastness, appearing, fading, appearing.

And within that movement, an order revealed itself: Intentions mattered.

Not as moral slogans, but as seeds.

Cruelty ripened into pain.

Generosity ripened into ease.

Delusion ripened into confusion.

Clarity ripened into peace.

Not always immediately.

Not in simple lines.

But inevitably, as surely as fire burns and gravity pulls.

And again compassion rose, deeper now, because the mind could see: no one was trapped by fate. But many were trapped by habit, by unexamined patterns repeated until they felt like identity.

The Second Watch completed itself without triumph.

Only understanding.

. . .

The Third Watch: The Root of the Knot

The night reached its deepest darkness, that hour when the world feels most distant from morning. And yet the mind was now closer than ever to what is real.

The third knowing arose: the ending of the fermentations, the deep outflows that keep the cycle turning.

Here the struggle was not against an enemy outside. It was against misunderstanding itself—the subtle reflex of "I" and "mine," the contraction that turns experience into possession, the grasping that turns feeling into craving, craving into clinging, clinging into becoming.

The mind watched these movements as they formed.

Not with hatred.

Not with panic.

With the calm precision of someone finally willing to see the mechanism of suffering without flinching.

And in that seeing, the structure of the Four Noble Truths emerged, not as philosophy, not as doctrine, but as direct architecture: suffering, its cause, its cessation, and the path leading to its end.[5]

What had been a lifetime of searching resolved itself into something simple and unbreakable: if suffering has a cause, it can end. If craving can be seen clearly, it can be released. If "self" is a construction, it can loosen.

And when that loosening completed itself, there was a kind of freedom that did not depend on conditions.

Not a bliss that must be protected.

Not a calm that must be maintained.

A release.

A knowing: Done.

. . .

Dawn

Then dawn began to gather, not suddenly, but the way truth gathers when it has nowhere left to be hidden.

Grey entered the horizon. Birds stirred. The Nerañjarā River caught the earliest light and returned it as a thin, trembling ribbon.

Siddhārtha opened his eyes.

The tree was still a tree.

The river still a river.

The world still the world.

And yet everything was different because the mind that met it was no longer bound in the old way.

In that stillness, the story of Siddhārtha—seeker, prince, ascetic—fell away.

And the Buddha, the awakened one, sat quietly in the morning as if awakening had never needed spectacle, only honesty, only clarity, only the courage to see.

~

ANALYSIS: THE NIGHT THE MIND STOPS FABRICATING

The night beneath the Bodhi tree is often described as the climax of the Buddha's life story. But its real significance lies not in drama, spectacle, or supernatural intervention. What unfolds here is something far more radical—and far more intimate: *the complete unveiling of how the mind constructs suffering, and how that construction finally comes to an end.*

Unlike earlier chapters, this is not a chapter about dreams in the ordinary sense. There are no symbolic animals, no prophetic images, no narrative omens. What appears instead is something more austere and more decisive: **direct knowledge** (*ñāṇa*), arising in a mind that no longer distorts what it sees.

From Symbol to Direct Seeing

Throughout the earlier chapters of this book, dreams function as mirrors of conditioning. They reveal how fear, desire, memory, and karmic momentum surface symbolically when the mind is not governed by conceptual control. Dreams, visions, and intuitions appear as *indirect* modes of knowing—ways the psyche registers truths it cannot yet articulate clearly.

Chapter Six marks a decisive shift. Here, symbolic mediation falls away. The Buddha does not *dream* the truth of suffering, rebirth, and liberation. He **sees** it.

The Pāli Canon describes this night through the framework of the **Three Watches of the Night**, each corresponding to a distinct mode of knowledge:

1 Recollection of past lives (*pubbenivāsānussatiñāṇa*)

2 Knowledge of beings passing on according to their actions (*cutūpapātañāṇa*)

3 Knowledge of the destruction of the taints (*āsavakkhayañāṇa*)

These are not presented as altered states, visions, or dreamlike reveries. They are forms of **direct cognition**, arising when the mind is fully collected, purified, and undistracted.

This distinction matters. It preserves a central doctrinal point of early Buddhism: *awakening is not gradual enlightenment, partial awakening, or something one slips in and out of.* It happens once, decisively, when ignorance is cut at the root.

The Real Drama of This Chapter

The drama of Chapter Six is not cinematic conflict. There are no battles to win, no external enemies to defeat.

The real drama is far subtler, and far more universal: *the mind confronting its own habit of fabrication.*

In the first watch, the mind sees continuity: life after life, identity after identity, each shaped by longing, fear, and attachment. This is not nostalgia or cosmic memory; it is the recognition that suffering has a history.

In the second watch, the mind sees pattern: beings rise and fall according to their actions, not by chance, fate, or divine will. Ethics is revealed not as a moral commandment, but as a structure.

In the third watch, the mind turns inward and sees the engine itself: craving, clinging, ignorance—the forces that perpetuate becoming.

At this point, the mind no longer argues with reality. It no longer seeks refuge in hope, denial, or metaphysical consolation. It sees the pattern so completely that the pattern loses its power. This is why this chapter stands at the pivot of the entire book:

• Earlier chapters explore how dreams reveal conditioning.

• This chapter shows what happens when conditioning is understood **at its root.**

• And from that understanding, release becomes not a hope or belief, but a lived certainty.

Dreams, Intuition, and Karmic Ripening (Interpretive Lens)

To integrate the dream-thread of this book with the stark clarity of the Bodhi-tree account, it is helpful to distinguish carefully between *symbolic intuition* and *liberating knowledge.*

Earlier in this book, I proposed—purely as an interpretive lens, not as doctrine—that some dreamlike episodes in Buddhist narrative may reflect sensitivity to karmic conditions approaching maturation. In such cases, understanding appears indirectly, clothed in symbol, mood, and image rather than clear liberating knowledge. What follows marks a decisive contrast. In the Bodhi-tree account, symbolic intuition gives way to direct seeing: there is no dream here, no veil of imagery, but unmediated knowledge of things as they have come to be.

The night beneath the Bodhi tree marks the end of this process. Here, there is no symbol left to interpret, no image left to decode. Karmic ripening culminates in *direct, irreversible insight.*

Ignorance does not subside temporarily. It does not retreat. It is extinguished.

This framing preserves doctrinal integrity while allowing dreams to remain meaningful within the broader narrative of long-term cultivation across many lives. Awakening is singular and final, but the conditions that make it possible unfold gradually, sometimes announcing themselves in subtle, symbolic ways long before clarity is complete.

Why This Matters for the Reader

The Buddha's awakening is not presented here as a mystical anomaly reserved for a single historical figure. It is presented as a *human possibility*, grounded in careful observation of the mind.

This chapter invites the reader to notice something essential:

- Much of ordinary life is spent reacting to mental fabrications.

- We bargain with impermanence.

- We seek comfort in stories the mind tells itself.

- We confuse insight with intuition, and intuition with truth.

The night beneath the Bodhi tree shows what happens when that process ends.

Not through force.

Not through belief.

But through understanding so complete that fabrication no longer arises.

Dreams have guided the narrative up to this point.

Here, they fall silent.

What remains is not emptiness, but clarity.

And from that clarity, a different way of being in the world becomes possible—one no longer driven by fear of loss, hunger for becoming, or confusion about what the mind is doing to itself.

This is why Chapter Six does not merely recount an awakening. It *demonstrates* what it means for the mind to stop dreaming reality and begin seeing it as it is.

CHAPTER SEVEN — THE ENDING OF THE HOUSE

Night still held Uruvelā in its vast, unbroken quiet.

The river moved without urgency, sliding over stones shaped smooth by centuries of surrender. The great fig tree stood unmoving, its roots gripping the earth with a patience older than memory.

Beneath it, Siddhārtha sat.

His body was steady, neither strained nor relaxed, as though it had finally learned how to rest inside itself.

The long night of seeing was drawing toward its deepest point.

The First Watch had opened memory beyond a single life. The Second had revealed the lawful movement of beings through birth and death. Now, in the final watch, nothing new needed to appear. What remained was to see clearly what had always been there.

∼

There was no struggle.

No voice challenged him.

No image rose to test him.

No temptation pressed forward to be resisted or overcome.

The mind had grown too still for spectacle.

Instead, there was a precise clarity, a seeing so intimate it felt quieter than thought.

He saw that experience continued to arise, sensations, sounds, the coolness of air on skin, the faint rhythm of breath, but nowhere within this flow was there anything that stood apart.

No watcher behind the seeing.

No owner behind the knowing.

No center from which experience radiated outward.

The assumption of self, so familiar, so ancient, did not assert itself.

Not because it was restrained.

Not because it was examined and dismissed.

But because *the conditions that once sustained it were no longer present*.

The mind did not *let go* of self. It saw that there had never been anything there to hold.

This seeing did not arrive as a thought.

It was not a conclusion.

Not a realization assembled from insight.

It was the *absence of misapprehension*.

Like a hand opening after discovering it was never gripping anything at all.

Dependent origination revealed itself completely, not as a teaching, but as structure:

Ignorance as condition.

Formations as condition.

Consciousness.

Name-and-form.

Contact.

Feeling.

Craving.

Clinging.

Becoming.

Birth.

Aging and death.

He saw it not as sequence but as simultaneity, a web of mutual support that collapsed when a single strand was removed.

When ignorance ceased, nothing followed.[1]

Not peace replacing turmoil.

Not bliss replacing pain.

But *the ending of the machinery itself*.

No craving arose.

No clinging formed.

No becoming found ground.

The process did not unwind.

It simply did not begin again.[2]

∼

This was not annihilation.

Nothing was destroyed.

The world did not vanish.

The body did not disappear.

The river did not stop flowing.

But the *error*, the fundamental misreading that turned movement into suffering, was no longer possible.

The mind stood free not because it had escaped experience, but because it no longer mistook experience for identity.

There was knowing without a knower. Seeing without a seer. Awareness without an owner.

The house of self, built and rebuilt across countless lives, had lost its foundation.

Not broken by force.

Not torn apart by effort.

Seen through.

∼

A verse arose naturally, not composed, not summoned, but released from the stillness itself:

Through many lives I wandered in saṁsāra, seeking the builder of this house. Painful is birth again and again.

The words did not echo.

They settled.

And with them, another knowing followed:

House-builder, you are seen. You shall build no house again. All your rafters are broken, your ridge-pole shattered. The mind has gone to the unconditioned. Craving is ended.[3]

The Dreaming Mind

This was not triumph. It was relief. A long, immeasurable relief.

Dawn approached quietly.

The sky lightened not with drama but with inevitability.

Birds stirred. Leaves trembled faintly. The river continued its path without pause or recognition.

Siddhārtha opened his eyes.

The world appeared exactly as it had before, and entirely different.

Forms were clear without being grasped. Sounds arose without demanding a response. The body breathed without reference to a self.

Nothing needed correction.

Nothing needed improvement.

The mind did not cling to peace.

Did not protect stillness.

Did not seek to preserve insight.

There was nothing left that could be lost.

He remained seated as the first sunlight touched the roots of the tree. The earth beneath him was cool, steady, unchanged. He placed his hand upon it, not as witness, not as invocation, but simply as contact.

This ground had always supported him.

Now, he understood why.

The long journey of becoming had ended.

Not in disappearance.

Not in transcendence.

But in *clarity so complete that suffering could no longer arise*.[4]

Siddhārtha had become the Buddha.

Awakened.

Unbound.

At peace.

And the world, unaware, unchanged, yet forever different, continued to turn.

∽

ANALYSIS: CHAPTER SEVEN: AWAKENING AS CESSATION, NOT EXPERIENCE

The awakening of the Buddha is often described in language that makes it sound like a final internal event—a last battle, a decisive insight, or a climactic moment of realization. But the early Buddhist texts point in a very different direction. What occurs beneath the Bodhi tree is not the appearance of something new, but the *irreversible disappearance of the conditions that make suffering possible at all*.[5]

Chapter Seven marks this turning with deliberate restraint. There is no psychological drama, no inner dialogue, no lingering struggle with doubt, desire, or selfhood. This is not because such forces are being heroically overcome in the final moment, but because *they no longer exist*.

This distinction is essential.

In early Buddhist doctrine, awakening is not a refined mental state. It is not a peak experience. It is not a heightened awareness that must be maintained. It is the *complete destruction of the roots of ignorance, craving, and conceit*.[6] When these roots are cut, they do not regenerate. There is no remainder.

The Dreaming Mind

That is why the texts speak of awakening in terms of **knowledge of destruction** (āsavakkhayañāṇa) rather than insight into processes still unfolding.[7] The taints are destroyed. They do not soften. They do not thin. They do not flicker and fade. They end.

Why Nothing "Arises" at Awakening

For modern readers, especially those shaped by psychological or therapeutic models, it can feel natural to imagine awakening as a moment where subtle traces of selfhood arise and are gently seen through. But this framing does not belong to early Buddhism.

The Pāli Canon is unambiguous: once Buddhahood is attained, *ignorance does not arise even faintly*.[8] Not as assumption. Not as habit. Not as echo. Why? Because ignorance is not merely suppressed; it is *uprooted*.

The same is true of conceit and aversion. These are not tendencies that slowly quiet down after enlightenment. They are eradicated.[9] The mind of a Buddha does not "notice" selfing—because there is no selfing to notice.

This is why Chapter Seven does not portray awakening as the mind watching subtle movements of "I-making" dissolve. That would imply that those movements still occur. Instead, the chapter presents awakening as *a structural collapse*: the conditions that once gave rise to self-reference simply fail to arise.

The Canon uses architectural metaphors for this moment. The Buddha speaks of the "house-builder"—craving—being seen and rendered powerless. The rafters are broken. The ridgepole shattered. The house cannot be rebuilt.[10]

What ends is not a belief. What ends is a *mechanism*.

Dependent Origination Seen in Reverse

A central insight of Chapter Seven is the reversal of dependent origination (*paṭiccasamuppāda*). Earlier chapters explore how experience is constructed—how perception, feeling, and craving shape both dreams and waking life. Here, that construction is seen *from the point where it fails to initiate.*

The Buddha does not merely understand dependent origination conceptually. He sees—directly—that when ignorance does not arise, the entire chain collapses:

• When ignorance ceases, formations cease

• When formations cease, consciousness does not establish

• When consciousness does not establish, name-and-form do not proliferate

• When name-and-form do not proliferate, suffering does not arise[11]

This is not an altered state. It is the **absence of a process**.

From the reader's perspective, this reframes awakening entirely. Liberation is not about maintaining insight. It is about *ending the conditions that require maintenance in the first place.*

Why This Is Not Emotional or Experiential

One of the most striking features of the Canon's awakening accounts is their emotional neutrality. There is no elation. No bliss narrative. No sense of personal achievement. This is not accidental.

Emotion, in Buddhist analysis, depends on appropriation—on experience being taken as "mine." When appropriation ends, emotion as grasping also ends.[12] What remains is clarity, equanimity, and compassion—but not as moods. As *modes of functioning.*

Chapter Seven reflects this by resisting sentimental language. The Buddha does not feel victorious. He is not relieved. He does not marvel at his own transformation. There is simply peace without ownership.

This is why the texts describe awakening as *nibbāna*, "cooling", rather than illumination or ecstasy.[13] The fires of greed, hatred, and delusion are extinguished. The metaphor is not ascent, but release.

The Dreaming Mind

Dreaming and the End of Fabrication

Throughout this book, dreams have served as a lens for understanding how the mind constructs meaning. Dreams show us, vividly, how worlds are fabricated from memory, emotion, and expectation. They reveal the mind's creative power.

Chapter Seven shows the other side of that coin.

Awakening is the point at which fabrication ends. Not temporarily. Not symbolically. Completely. The mind no longer dreams itself into existence—neither at night nor during waking life.

This does not mean perception stops. The Buddha still sees, hears, walks, teaches. But experience is no longer organized around a center. There is no narrative self-woven through sensation. The dream has ended, not because it was exposed as false, but because the conditions that produced it are gone.

This is why awakening is irreversible. You cannot return to a dream once the machinery that generates it has been dismantled.

Why This Chapter Is the Pivot of the Book

Earlier chapters show how dreams, intuitions, and symbolic experiences reflect karmic conditioning. They show how the mind senses truth before it can articulate it. They show how meaning ripens over time.

Chapter Seven shows what happens when that ripening is complete.

There is no longer symbolism. No longer intuition. No longer preparation. The work is finished. The path has done what it was meant to do and is laid down.

For the reader, this chapter quietly reorients the entire project of spiritual practice. It suggests that liberation is not about becoming more insightful, more aware, or more refined. It is about ending the need to become anything at all.

That is why the Buddha's first words after awakening are not a proclamation of identity, but a statement of cessation: birth is ended, the holy life fulfilled, what had to be done has been done.[14]

Nothing is added. Everything unnecessary is gone.

∼

Why This Chapter Matters for the Reader

At first glance, Chapter Seven may seem distant from ordinary life.

It describes a state so complete, so final, that most readers will never experience it directly. The Buddha's awakening is not something to imitate, rehearse, or gradually approximate. It happens once, and it ends the very conditions that make ordinary experience feel personal, conflicted, and incomplete.

So why dwell here?

Because this chapter reveals something essential about how suffering operates right now.

The Buddha's awakening matters not because readers are meant to replicate it, but because it exposes, with absolute clarity, the mechanism by which distress is continuously manufactured in everyday life.

The chapter shows that suffering does not come from events themselves, but from a subtle process that precedes reaction:

• the reflex of "this is happening to me"

• the assumption that experience requires an owner

• the habit of organizing sensations around a center

Readers may recognize this not as philosophy, but as lived experience. The tightening in the chest when criticized. The mental recoil from discomfort. The constant background effort to secure, defend, or explain oneself.

Chapter Seven shows what happens when that mechanism is absent, not softened, not managed, not reframed, but *no longer operating at all.*

This has immediate relevance.

Even without awakening, readers can begin to notice that:

• distress intensifies when experience is appropriated as "mine"

• peace appears when that appropriation loosens, even briefly

• the mind fabricates continuity and identity far more often than it needs to

In this sense, the Buddha's awakening functions as a *diagnostic lens*, not a spiritual demand.

It clarifies what freedom would require, and therefore what suffering depends on.

The chapter also corrects a common misunderstanding: that liberation is about achieving a better version of oneself. Chapter Seven makes clear that liberation is not about improvement, but **about release**, the release of a pattern that has been unconsciously repeated for a very long time.

The path is revealed not as striving toward something new, but as seeing clearly what is already in place.

The question is no longer: *How do I become more awakened?* But rather: *What is being assumed, moment by moment, that does not need to be assumed at all?*

Chapter Seven does not answer that question with advice.

It answers it by showing, with rare clarity, what the end of assumption looks like.

And once that is seen, even from a distance, the reader can never quite look at their own experience in the same way again.

CHAPTER EIGHT — THE WORLD AS IT IS SEEN

The early light rested gently on the foothills. Mist lingered among the tall grasses, lifting in slow, quiet currents, as though the earth itself were releasing the last breath of night.

The Buddha walked alone. His steps were even, unhurried, the steps of one whose seeing no longer reached forward to secure what had never promised to remain.

Birdsong threaded the cool air. The sky carried the first warmth of dawn. The scent of water and soil rose softly from the ground.

Nothing in the morning was unusual. And yet, for a mind no longer caught by the appearance of solidity, everything revealed itself without disguise.

He paused beneath a fig tree.

A single droplet gathered at the curve of a leaf, hung briefly, then released.

It fell.

It struck the soil and disappeared at once, leaving behind only a darkened trace.

For most, the moment would pass unnoticed, one small movement in a world already full of movement.

But to him, the falling of the droplet mirrored a truth spoken again and again in the earliest days after awakening: that all conditioned things arise dependent on causes and vanish when those causes no longer hold.

He had spoken once of the five aggregates as appearances without weight, form like foam, feeling like a bubble, perception like a mirage, not to deny the world, but to reveal how lightly it rests upon conditions.[1]

The droplet had fallen.

The droplet had vanished.

Only change remained.

A breeze passed through the leaves.

Light trembled along their edges.

The world shimmered, not with wonder, but with impermanence seen clearly.

He walked on.

The path curved gently between trees whose shadows shifted as the sun climbed higher. The forest floor was layered with fallen leaves, their colors softened, their edges curling inward, quiet witnesses to the same truth spoken by the droplet.

Nothing held its shape. Even the body that walked, feet pressing into earth, muscles adjusting, breath rising and falling, changed moment by moment, responding to slope, to balance, to effort.

There was no owner behind the movement. Only movement.

Ahead, the land opened into a valley washed in early light.

Mist lifted in pale ribbons. A river caught the sun and scattered it in shifting fragments.

He stood at the edge of the clearing. The world before him appeared as it always had, paths and water, hills and trees, the ordinary architecture of living. Yet solidity no longer deceived.

In one discourse, he had described how beings are drawn toward appearances as a traveler chases a mirage, mistaking shimmer for water.[2]

The error was not seeing. The error was believing what flickers to be stable.

To see change clearly was not to withdraw from the world. It was to meet it without false assurance.

He continued walking.

∼

The forest thickened.

Water loosened itself over unseen stones. Sunlight filtered down in thin, wavering lines that shifted with each breath of wind.

He moved beneath an arch of branches, his steps light, unresistant.

This quiet seeing, this steady awareness of change unfolding moment by moment, was neither dream nor illusion. And yet it shared the same fleeting quality.

Later generations would speak of conditioned things as dreamlike, brief, ungraspable, unable to satisfy, not because they were unreal, but because they could not be held.[3]

Those words would travel far, across centuries and lands. But their root lay here, in what had already been seen beneath the Bodhi tree: that experience arises, displays itself vividly, and dissolves without remainder.

Leaves shifted color as the sun rose.

Light moved.

Shadow followed.

Nothing promised to remain.

This was not cause for sorrow. It was simply the way things are.

And truth, seen without resistance, was release.

The path narrowed, curling between stones softened by moss and time.

Even in stillness, movement lived everywhere, in the sway of branches, the settling of dust, the quiet hum of insects beneath the leaves.

Some who had approached him had once believed that change meant danger, that instability was a flaw in the world.

But he had spoken plainly: all conditioned things are inconstant, subject to alteration, unable to endure even for the blink of an eye.[4] For those who turned away, this truth felt unsettling, like ground that would not stay firm. For those who stayed with it, it opened like a gate.

He paused where the forest thinned.

The valley returned to view, villages already awake.

Smoke lifted from hearths. Figures moved through fields. Children ran across the dust.

Life unfolded as it always had.

And yet, from here, it carried the lightness of a dream, not because it was false, but because it was fleeting.

Later texts would speak openly of this dreamlike nature, saying that phenomena rise and vanish as swiftly as visions in sleep.[5]

These were expansions, clarifications, not departures.

The foundation had already been laid.

He stood quietly, watching the ordinary movement of lives shaped by causes they rarely saw.

Nothing stayed the same from one breath to the next.

And yet, everything continued.

When he turned back toward the forest, sal trees rose around him, their pale blossoms drifting downward in soft spirals.

Petals gathered on the path like silent snowfall.

He paused before one.

Its edges were thin, already beginning to curl.

He had taught that feelings arise and fade like bubbles on water, that perception misleads like heat shimmering over sand.[6]

The blossom reflected the same truth, not as doctrine, but as presence.

There was no need to explain it.

Seeing was enough.

For those who seek certainty in what changes, the world feels unstable.

For those who understand change, the world grows light.

He continued on.

The monastery appeared ahead.

Monks moved through the courtyard in measured rhythms, sweeping, carrying water, preparing the day.

Each gesture revealed the play of conditions: body adjusting to effort, feeling rising and falling, intention shaping movement.

No action stood alone.

He had said that the aggregates are like a magic trick, convincing,

yet empty of substance when seen clearly.[7]

Their instability was not a problem.

It was the opening.

Inside the meditation hall, breath rose and fell.

Thoughts appeared and vanished without trace.

Perceptions flickered.

Sounds dissolved as they arose.

No one needed to push them away.

They fell on their own.

He had spoken of perception as a reflection, easily altered, never fixed.[8]

Here, that truth unfolded without words.

Later teachers would say that insight is like waking from a dream, not because the world disappears, but because misperception ends.[9]

The Buddha opened his eyes.

Outside, a petal touched the earth and came to rest, complete in its briefness.

He rose and walked on, the morning opening before him in quiet, ever-changing light.

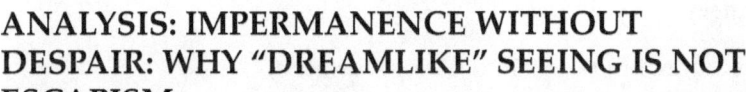

ANALYSIS: IMPERMANENCE WITHOUT DESPAIR: WHY "DREAMLIKE" SEEING IS NOT ESCAPISM

Chapter 8 is intentionally quiet.

After the high drama of renunciation, the intensities of striving, the night of awakening, and the threshold where the inner architecture of suffering is understood, this chapter does something radical: it refuses spectacle. It lingers instead on a droplet falling from a leaf, petals gathering on a path, monks lifting water, a mind noticing the rise and fall of breath.

That restraint is not a stylistic lull. It is the teaching.

Because one of the most difficult shifts in Buddhist practice—and one of the most relevant shifts for a modern reader—is learning to recognize that insight is not an event you admire from a distance. It is a way of seeing that changes how you relate to ordinary life.

1) "Like foam, like a bubble": the early Buddhist grammar of dreamlike appearance

The chapter's core textual anchor is the Buddha's use of image-language to describe the aggregates—form, feeling, perception, formations, consciousness—as unstable and insubstantial in the sense of being *unreliable*, not in the sense of being nonexistent. In the *Phena Sutta*, the Buddha compares these components of experience to foam, bubbles, mirages, and illusion-like displays.[10]

This is crucial to the book's overall theme. The dream thread is not included to romanticize dreams or treat them as mystical announcements. It is included because dreams are a lived demonstration of what Buddhist analysis claims about all conditioned experience:

• it arises dependent on conditions,

• it convinces us while it is occurring,

• it changes,

• and it cannot be grasped into lasting satisfaction.

Dreams are not "special" in Buddhism because they reveal a hidden reality elsewhere. They are special because they make the logic of experience obvious: we see how quickly a world can form, how persuasive it can feel, and how quickly it collapses.

Waking life is not identical to a dream, but it shares the same *structure of conditioned appearance*.

This chapter is where that implication becomes experiential rather than conceptual.

2) Impermanence isn't the problem, clinging is

Modern readers often meet "impermanence" as a gloomy thesis: *everything changes, therefore nothing matters.* But the early discourses are more precise and more psychologically sophisticated. They do not argue that because things pass, they are meaningless. They argue that because things pass, *clinging is structurally misaligned with reality,* and that misalignment produces stress.

This is one reason the chapter keeps returning to small images: the droplet, the petal, the shifting light.

Not to be poetic for poetry's sake, but because this is how impermanence becomes real: not through slogans, but through contact.

A modern reader knows change intimately:

• relationships change,

• health changes,

• moods shift,

• work conditions turn,

• your "future self" becomes someone you didn't predict.

The suffering isn't that life changes. The suffering is the constant demand, often unconscious, that life *shouldn't.*

Chapter 8 is quietly training the reader's nervous system to accept what the intellect already knows. The droplet falls, and the mind sees: *this is the way it is.* When that seeing matures, the heart stops arguing with reality. That's not resignation. It's freedom from futile friction.

3) The mirage problem: why the mind can't stop mistaking shimmer for substance

The Buddha often describes how the mind is "captured" by appearances —how it runs after what flashes before the senses as if that flashing could finally deliver security. The chapter invokes the mirage imagery preserved in the suttas: beings chase what appears alluring, assuming it can provide lasting satisfaction.[11]

For a contemporary reader, this is less about deserts and literal mirages and more about:

• scrolling for relief,

• chasing the next purchase,

• replaying arguments,

• needing certainty before acting,

• needing reassurance before resting.

The mind repeatedly assumes: *If I can just get the right condition, I'll be okay.*

And life repeatedly demonstrates: conditions shift.

Chapter 8 sits directly on that pressure point. It doesn't moralize about desire. It simply shows how the world behaves when seen cleanly: it is not stable enough to serve as a foundation for identity or lasting safety.

4) Why "dreamlike" is not nihilism: two traditions, one caution

This chapter also carefully distinguishes early and later voices.

In the early discourses, the language is restrained: foam, bubbles, mirages, illusions.[12] Later Mahāyāna texts become explicit, declaring that conditioned phenomena are "like a dream."[13] That later emphasis can be misread—especially in modern contexts—as implying that nothing is real, therefore ethics and compassion don't matter.

But the Buddhist point is sharper: because experience is conditioned and passing, it is *ethically consequential*. You can't freeze a life into safety, so the question becomes: what kind of intention do you plant into what is passing?

Even when phenomena are described as dreamlike, Buddhism does not license indifference. It makes compassion urgent—because beings suffer precisely by clinging to what cannot hold them.

Chapter 8 can therefore be read as a corrective to two modern extremes:

• the anxious grasping for permanence (the attempt to secure the unsecurable), and

• the cynical dismissal of meaning (the attempt to avoid vulnerability by calling everything "fake").

This chapter refuses both. It keeps the world intact, villagers working, monks sweeping, petals falling, while shifting the reader's relationship to it.

5) Where the dream theme lands in the reader's body

A subtle achievement of this chapter is that it relocates "dreams" from being occasional nighttime events to being a metaphor for how the mind habitually constructs experience. The chapter does not claim waking life is literally a dream. It suggests something more practical:

If you look closely, the mind is always producing a version of reality:

• selecting details,

• highlighting threats,

• inventing continuity,

• narrating identity,

• predicting outcomes,

• projecting meaning.

That constructive function is not a mistake, it is how cognition works.

The mistake is forgetting it's happening.

Dreams help you notice this because they are construction without external constraint. But waking life has construction too—just anchored to sensory input and social reinforcement.

For a modern reader, this is immediately relevant. The raw facts of life do not primarily cause many forms of suffering today, but by the mind's insistence that its interpretation is reality itself. Chapter 8 teaches a gentler possibility:

You can experience the world *without insisting on solidity where there is none.*

6) The practical takeaway: what changes if you truly understand "things pass"?

If this chapter is doing its job, the reader finishes it with a different orientation, not simply a different idea.

Here's what it can begin to change in modern life:

- **Less catastrophizing.** If you see thoughts and emotions as events that arise and pass, they lose some of their authority.

- **Less compulsive fixing.** Not everything that feels urgent is actually urgent; many urges are just waves.

- **More intimacy with life.** When you stop demanding permanence, you can meet what is here more fully—because you're not bracing against its ending.

- **Cleaner ethics.** If outcomes are unstable, intention becomes central: what do you plant into change?

- **A different relationship to grief.** You still feel loss, but the mind stops adding the secondary suffering of *this shouldn't be happening.*

This is why Chapter 8 matters. It's not a philosophical interlude. It's the lived training of insight: seeing the world as it is, without collapsing into despair, and without clinging to illusions of control.

. . .

7) How this chapter functions in the book's arc

Structurally, Chapter 8 is a hinge:

• Earlier chapters treat dreams as symbol, omen, and inner atmosphere shaping action.

• Chapters 6–7 show the culmination of practice: the mind seeing through the machinery of suffering.

• Chapter 8 shows what happens after: not fireworks, but *integration*.

Awakening is not merely an experience. It is a stabilization of view. It changes how a person walks, watches a droplet fall, sees a monk lift a bucket, hears birds in the trees. The chapter teaches the reader, implicitly: the measure of insight is how it meets the ordinary.

And that is exactly why the chapter is modern.

Because modern people are not mostly suffering from a lack of dramatic mystical events. They are suffering from relentless mental construction and the exhaustion of trying to make life hold still. Chapter 8 offers a different way: not to escape the world, but to stop demanding from it what it cannot give.

CHAPTER NINE — NIMITTA, VISIONS, AND THE SHIFTING TEXTURE OF CONSCIOUSNESS

Night settled gently over the monastery. Not as a sudden darkness, but as a gradual softening, the light thinning, the edges of the world loosening as the sun withdrew behind distant hills.

In the courtyard, oil lamps burned low, their flames wavering as if uncertain whether to rise or rest. Each lamp cast a narrow pool of gold onto the packed earth, circles of warmth surrounded by deepening shadow.

Beyond the walls, the forest held its breath. The sal trees stood unmoving, their leaves barely stirring, as though the night itself were listening.

Inside the meditation hall, the air was cool and still.

Monks entered quietly, one by one, the sound of bare feet on smooth stone barely audible. Robes brushed against woven mats. Bodies settled. Spines straightened.

The ordinary movements of preparation ended.

Silence gathered.

The Buddha entered last.

The Dreaming Mind

There was nothing remarkable in the way he walked, no display, no pause meant to be noticed.

And yet, as he crossed the threshold, the atmosphere shifted.

Not because he willed it, but because the mind of one who has fully understood no longer disturbs the space it enters.

He took his seat near the center of the hall.

At once, the room seemed to deepen, as if sound itself had learned how to rest.

At first, there was only breath.

A quiet rising.

A quiet falling.

The body sat as something placed down and no longer adjusted.

The muscles released their vigilance.

The face softened.

The chest moved with an ease that needed no instruction.

Shadows along the walls shifted subtly as the lamp flames breathed.

Light trembled.

Then steadied.

For a long while, nothing else occurred.

No vision.

No insight.

No change worth naming.

This, too, was practice.

Then—without announcement—the quality of attention shifted.

Not the breath itself.

Not the body.

But the *way* the breath was known.

Awareness gathered.

The boundary between breathing and knowing the breath grew thin,

then thinner still.

The mind was no longer moving toward its object.

It was resting *with* it.

This was the terrain the early discourses describe with great restraint: the settling of attention, the unification of mind, the quieting of the senses.

Nothing supernatural.

Nothing symbolic.

Just the mind no longer scattering itself.

At first, the signs were almost imperceptible.

A faint brightness behind the closed eyelids, not an image, not a form, just a subtle clarity, as though attention had cleaned its own lens.

A lightness appeared in the face and head, as if effort had been quietly set down.

The breath itself seemed luminous.

In the early texts, this natural clarity is called *pabhassara*, the mind's brightness when defilements are absent or temporarily stilled.[1]

Not a vision.

Not a revelation.

Not something to be pursued.

The Dreaming Mind

Simply what the mind is when it is not obstructed.

The Buddha had spoken of this often, careful to emphasize that luminosity is not awakening.

It is not freedom.

It is only clarity, beautiful, unstable, and impermanent.

Even this must not be clung to.

As the stillness deepened, perception softened.

Sounds from outside, a distant bird, the faint crack of cooling wood, no longer pulled attention outward.

They arose and vanished like ripples that leave no wake.

The usual markers of experience lost their urgency.

Then another shift appeared.

The commentarial tradition would later call it *nimitta*—a mental "sign" that arises when concentration stabilizes.[2]

But in the Canon itself, the treatment is restrained.

No mythology.

No promise.

Only observation.

When the mind becomes unified, it begins to perceive its own collectedness.

Tonight, a gentle radiance seemed to suffuse the hall.

It did not illuminate objects.

It did not cast shadows.

It had no clear edge.

It was felt more than seen, a steady presence, unburdened, quiet.

In other discourses, monks described such experiences in different ways: a star before the mind, a glowing disk, a soft mist of light.[3]

The forms varied.

The cause did not.

The mind had stopped scattering itself.

For those unfamiliar with such territory, this stage of practice can feel disorienting.

The world no longer behaves as expected.

Space seems to widen or contract. The body feels distant, or faint, or absent altogether.

The Buddha did not deny this. He explained it.

When attention no longer relies on the senses for orientation, perception becomes fluid.

This is not illusion.

It is the mind no longer anchored to its usual reference points.

Tonight, even the breath grew subtle, so refined it seemed to disappear.[4]

This was not danger.

This was absorption.

A collecting so complete that effort itself had fallen silent.

Outside the hall, the night continued its work, dew forming on leaves, the earth cooling.

Inside, the mind rested like a lake untouched by wind.

At times, such stillness can give rise to unusual bodily perceptions.

The Dreaming Mind

In some suttas, monks reported the sense that the hall tilted, or that the body floated above the ground.[5]

The Buddha addressed these calmly.

They were not signs of progress.

Nor signs of error.

They were distortions—natural effects of perception loosening from its habitual anchors.[6]

When sound, body, and thought release their grip, the mind reconfigures how it maps experience.

The crucial factor was not what appeared, but whether awareness remained steady.

Dreamlike does not mean deluded. What matters is clarity.

As the mind remained balanced, the nimitta neither intensified nor elaborated.

It did not promise.

It did not speak.

It simply remained for a time, reflecting the mind's collected state.

Thoughts became weightless.

Feelings softened.

Perception floated without fastening itself to form or meaning.

This is the threshold described in the discourses before the deep absorptions—the jhānas—fully establish themselves.[7]

Later traditions would describe this territory with dream imagery: standing at the edge of sleep, waking inside a dream, hovering before form arises.

The Buddha himself was more cautious.

Lights, signs, even profound stillness, none of these were liberation.

To cling to them was to turn away from the path.

Even clarity must be released.

Even beauty must be known as impermanent.

Time moved gently in the hall.

The lamps burned lower.

Shadows thinned.

The collective breath rose and fell like a slow tide.

Gradually, the nimitta softened.

The radiance dimmed without resistance.

The body returned—the weight of legs, the warmth of hands, the subtle movement of air against skin.

Perception reassembled itself around familiar contours.

The Buddha opened his eyes.

The hall was unchanged.

Yet everything was seen more precisely.

No vision.

No proclamation.

Just understanding.

He rose quietly from his seat.

Outside, the night had begun to thin.

A pale light touched the horizon, neither dark nor day.

One star remained in the sky, a reminder that luminosity does not depend on effort.

He stepped into the courtyard.

The air was cool.

The earth firm beneath his feet.

The world was neither dream nor refuge, only changing phenomena known clearly for what they are.

And that seeing was enough.

∼

ANALYSIS: NIMITTA, DREAMLIKE PERCEPTION, AND THE MIND THAT KNOWS ITSELF

In this chapter, nothing supernatural occurs.

No prophecy is delivered.

No vision reveals a hidden realm.

And yet, something profoundly important is shown.

The meditation hall becomes a laboratory in which the Buddha demonstrates how *perception itself changes when the mind grows still*. What begins as ordinary awareness gradually reveals a different texture—softer, brighter, less anchored to the familiar boundaries of body and world. This shift is not imagination; it is the mind encountering its own processes with fewer distortions.[8]

When concentration deepens, the world does not disappear. It becomes *less insistent*. Edges blur. Sounds lose their pull. The body recedes into the background. Experience begins to resemble a dream, not because it is unreal, but because its usual solidity no longer convinces.[9]

This resemblance is not accidental. The Buddha understood that *dreaming and deep concentration share structural similarities:* both arise when sensory input quiets and the mind's constructive activity becomes more visible. The difference is that in meditation, awareness remains steady. One does not fall *into* the dreamlike state; one *witnesses* it.[10]

The Meaning of Nimitta

The appearance of nimitta, the meditative "sign" described in this chapter, marks a critical threshold. In the early texts, nimitta is not treated as a mystical vision. It is simply what becomes apparent when attention stabilizes and distraction fades. The mind, no longer scattered, reflects its own collected state as light, clarity, or spaciousness.[11]

Nimitta is a condition, not a realization. It arises, abides briefly, and passes away like every other conditioned experience. To cling to it is to reintroduce grasping at the very moment when grasping has begun to loosen.[12]

The dreamlike quality described in this chapter, the sense of floating, widening, or spatial distortion, belongs to the same category. These are not errors or hallucinations. They are *perceptual adjustments* that occur when the mind withdraws from its habitual anchors. The Buddha explained them plainly as consequences of unification, not as messages or omens.[13]

Dreamlike Does Not Mean Unreal

A crucial distinction must be made here, especially for modern readers.

When Buddhism describes perception as dreamlike, it does **not** mean that the world is illusory in the sense of being nonexistent. Rather, it means that experience is **constructed, unstable, and dependent on**

conditions. Just as a dream feels real while it lasts, waking perception feels solid while the mind remains entangled in habit.[14]

The Buddha's famous comparisons: form as foam, feeling as a bubble, perception as a mirage, consciousness as a magic trick, are not poetic exaggerations. They are precise descriptions of how experience behaves when examined closely.[15] Dreams dramatize this instability. Meditation reveals it quietly.

In this way, Chapter 9 completes a subtle arc that has been developing throughout the book. Earlier chapters explored dreams as symbolic expressions of karmic patterning. Here, meditation reveals the same truth from the opposite direction: when the mind grows still, even waking life displays the same fleeting, constructed nature as a dream.

Why This Matters for the Modern Reader

For a contemporary reader, this teaching is unexpectedly practical.

Modern life trains attention to fragment, accelerate, and harden around identity. We are taught, subtly and constantly, that experience must be controlled, optimized, and secured. Meditation, as presented here, offers a radical alternative: *see how experience actually behaves when control relaxes.*

When the mind no longer grasps for stability, it discovers that impermanence is not a threat. It is simply the nature of things. The dreamlike quality of perception does not undermine meaning; it frees it from the burden of false permanence.

This insight explains why Buddhist practice does not aim to replace one version of reality with another. It aims to remove the confusion that makes reality feel heavier than it is. *Nimitta*, dreamlike perception, and luminous calm are not destinations. They are signposts indicating that the mind is beginning to see clearly.

The Place of This Chapter in the Book

Up to this point, dreams have functioned as narrative and symbol. After this point, they will become sites of practice—places where awareness may continue even as ordinary perception dissolves.

But before that exploration can begin, the reader must understand something essential: the dreamlike quality of experience is not confined to sleep. It is woven into perception itself. Meditation simply makes this visible.

By the end of the chapter, the Buddha returns from stillness without fanfare. Nothing has changed, and everything has. The world remains. The mind sees it differently. The dream has not been rejected. It has been understood.

And understanding, in this tradition, is enough.

CHAPTER TEN — DREAM YOGA BEFORE DREAM YOGA

Night arrived the way incense arrives, not as a sudden thing, but as a gradual softening of everything that once felt sharp. The last warmth of sunset drained from the sky until the air turned the color of deep blue ink. Palm leaves swayed, casting slow shadows across the sandy courtyard. Somewhere beyond the outer wall, the forest held itself still, as if the world, too, were learning how to listen.

Chanting ended. Not with a final flourish, but with a thinning, voices tapering into silence the way ripples taper into a pond.

Monks rose. Robes brushed mats. Feet moved softly across earth.

A few lamps remained, small, low flames holding their circles of gold against the widening dark.

The monastery did not "go to sleep." It changed texture.

The day released its grip.

The night drew close.

And the mind, freed from a thousand outward pulls, began to show itself.

Inside his dwelling, the Buddha sat. Not in formal meditation now, not posed as an emblem of holiness, but simply seated in ease, as natural as a tree resting in its own shade.

His posture was steady. His breath quiet. And the stillness around him was not empty; it was awake.

This was the hour when teaching often happened without being called teaching.

No discourse.

No debate.

No explanation.

Only the visible way an awakened mind meets the end of a day without clutching at it.

A young monk approached, bowed, and sat down a short distance away.

He did not come to ask. He came to train.

To watch how the Buddha moved through the liminal hour when waking begins to loosen and sleep begins to gather.

The Buddha lifted his gaze briefly.

In another setting, recorded in the discourses, he speaks of reviewing one's day with clarity.[1]

Not to punish the mind with regret, and not to inflate it with pride, but to see plainly what was done, what was felt, what was carried.

Tonight, he did not speak those words aloud.

He showed them.

The way he adjusted his robe—complete. The way he shifted his weight—unhurried. The way one moment ended before the next began.

For the early community, night was not a void in the training.

The Dreaming Mind

Mindfulness, the Buddha taught, was to be cultivated in every posture: walking, standing, sitting, and lying down.[2]

The body changes position; awareness does not have to vanish with it.

And so, before sleep, the disciple was encouraged to shape the mind gently, to incline it the way one inclines a lamp toward a darkened corner.

Not through force. Through care.

If the last thoughts of the day are scattered, sharp, resentful, hungry—sleep receives them, and dreams inherit their taste.

If the last thoughts of the day are settled, bright, harmless—the night is entered with a different kind of mind.

This is not superstition. It is causality. A mind does not become new at the moment the eyes close. It continues.

The Buddha rose. He placed the lamp nearer the wall, not to brighten the room, only to keep the edges visible. He prepared a mat—thin, plain, sufficient—a place large enough for the body, no more. Then he lay down on his right side—the lion posture described in the texts.[3] One foot rested lightly upon the other. One hand supported the head. The other lay along the body as simply as a branch lying along the ground.

The posture was not symbolic. It was practical. It carried no drama.

And yet to the young monk watching, it felt like instruction made visible: Even rest can be entered without carelessness.

In the discourses, the tradition preserves the theme of entering and leaving sleep mindfully—a continuity of awareness rather than a collapse into dullness.[4] No one is being asked to "defeat sleep." Only to meet it without abandoning the mind.

The Buddha's eyes closed. But sleep did not fall on him like a curtain.

The air in the room held a thin brightness, not from the lamp, but from presence.

A threshold state lingered—neither full waking nor dreaming—a soft wakefulness in which perception thins but knowing remains.[5]

The young monk breathed quietly, feeling the strangeness of it: how the mind could soften without falling into confusion, how it could relax without sinking, how it could enter the night without being swallowed by it.

Outside, the monastery darkened. Huts became silhouettes. Paths disappeared into shadow. The forest beyond the wall became a single mass of quiet.

Some monks slept deeply. Some slept lightly. Some turned from side to side, the day's residue still moving in them.

But in one corner of the grounds, a monk remained awake—not from restlessness, but from intention.

He walked slowly beneath the trees, feeling the earth under his feet.

Fatigue was present. The body wanted release. But the mind did not have to grow foggy just because the day was ending.

The early discourses preserve instructions for cultivating wholesome mental tone, including the steadying of the mind as the day declines.[6] The point is not to "keep awake," but to avoid the thickening haze that turns consciousness dull and unobservant.

He entered the meditation hall and sat down.

The hall smelled of woven mats, old wood, and oil from lamps.

Darkness behind the eyelids, at first, only darkness. Then the mind began its familiar unwinding. A thought from the day. A phrase remembered. A small irritation replayed. A moment of craving. A flash of embarrassment. A desire to fix what could not be fixed. All of it rose because night is honest.

The Dreaming Mind

When the world quiets, the mind grows louder. And here the training begins: not to fight thought, not to drown it, but to know it.

He watched the waves.

They rose.

They fell.

They weakened.

Then something else appeared, not story, not memory, but texture. A faint glow behind the eyelids. A widening sense of space. A softness at the edge of attention as though the mind were turning inward like a river finding its underground channel.

The Buddha's training in mindfulness includes knowing the mind in all conditions, even when lying down, even when drifting toward sleep.[7] This is subtle work.

Most people only notice that they "fell asleep." They do not notice how it happened. They do not notice the hinge.

The monk noticed the hinge.

Perception flickered. The sense of body softened, as though gentle hands were erasing the outline of the limbs. Thought grew porous. Images rose without intention, a fragment of a face, a suggestion of a place, a color with no object.

Then dissolved.

Then returned in another form.

This was not yet dreaming.

It was the border thinning.

A living demonstration of what the Buddha taught repeatedly: the mind is conditioned, shaped by causes, shaped by contact, habit, tendency, and everything conditioned changes.[8]

Sleep is not a disappearance. It is a shift in conditions. And in that shift, the mind reveals how easily it makes a world.

Then the transition.

Not dramatic.

Not announced.

A small click in the machinery.

A scene formed—vague outlines, movement without weight, a place that felt real without being tethered to the senses.

The mind had begun to dream.

Most beings enter this realm unaware, carried by momentum.

But the monk's earlier mindfulness followed the transition like a thread—thin, delicate, almost invisible, yet present.

He saw the forming.

He saw the dissolving.

He saw the way a world appears without anyone building it.

In dreams, the mind's craftsmanship is exposed.

Fear becomes landscape.

Desire becomes narrative.

Memory becomes present tense.

Identity becomes costume.

And the strangest thing, the most ordinary thing, is how quickly the dream-self believes:

This is me.

This is mine,

This is happening to me.

But tonight, that belief did not fully harden.

The monk's awareness did not control the dream. It did not command it. It simply knew: *This is forming. This is changing. This is not owned.*

The dream loosened.

Images softened, as if the mind were tiring of pretending solidity.

A brief clarity flashed—not light, not vision, but understanding.

Then, naturally, awareness returned to the quiet pulse of breath.

The dream thinned.

Sleep continued.

Mindfulness had entered the night.

At dawn, he awoke.

The hall was cool.

The lamps had burned down.

The world outside was still grey, birds not yet loud with morning.

Nothing spectacular had happened.

No miracle.

No prophecy.

No power gained.

And yet something had shifted.

He had seen how consciousness reorganizes itself. How it withdraws from the senses and begins to paint. How a self can appear and disappear without a core behind it.

Early Buddhism does not promise mastery over dreams. It offers something deeper: The possibility that awareness does not have to be interrupted, that it can follow the mind through its changing states the way moonlight follows water.

Where awareness reaches, freedom can follow.

And the night—so often treated as blankness—becomes, quietly, another field of understanding.

∽

ANALYSIS: WHAT EARLY BUDDHISM ACTUALLY TEACHES ABOUT SLEEP, DREAMS, AND NIGHT PRACTICE

Chapter Ten is important because it clarifies something many modern readers assume incorrectly: that early Buddhism either ignores dreams, treats sleep as irrelevant, or reserves night consciousness for later "esoteric" systems.

The early discourses do not teach dream yoga in the Tibetan sense—there is no instruction to manipulate dream imagery or to engineer lucidity. But early Buddhism *does* treat the transition into sleep as a legitimate arena for mindfulness and understanding.

1) Mindfulness "in all postures" includes the night

The foundational instructions on mindfulness explicitly include all postures, including lying down.[9] This matters because it frames sleep not as a spiritual "off switch," but as another changing condition that can be known.

Chapter Ten's core claim is simple: the mind does not become new at bedtime. It continues along causal grooves—carrying emotion, habit, and intention into the night.

That is why the state of mind before sleep is emphasized in early training. The point is not moralism; it is cause and effect.

2) The canon does not teach dream yoga—yet it plants the root

A common modern reading goes like this:

* Dream yoga is Tibetan; therefore, early Buddhism has nothing comparable.

That conclusion is too crude.

While the Pāli Canon does not teach dream yoga as a system, it repeatedly emphasizes continuity of mindfulness and knowledge of mind-states (including subtle ones). The "skill" presented in Chapter Ten is not control inside dreams. It is recognition of transition—the capacity to notice drifting, dullness, and the mind's re-patterning as sleep approaches.

Later dream yoga traditions build technique and structure on top of this. But the underlying insight is already present: consciousness changes lawfully, and the changing can be known.

3) Why the threshold before sleep is psychologically revealing

For modern readers, the most practical point of Chapter Ten is this: the minutes before sleep often reveal what the day has concealed.

When stimulation drops and the external world quiets, unresolved material rises—memories, anxieties, cravings, self-narratives. This is not an error; it is what happens when the mind no longer has daytime distractions to lean on.

Early Buddhism does not tell you to interpret these materials as prophecy. It invites you to understand them as conditioning, patterns that arise dependent on causes.

And this is where dreams become spiritually relevant: not because they are magical, but because they show how quickly the mind manufactures a world and a self.

4) Why this chapter matters for the modern reader

This chapter is relevant because it offers a workable middle ground between two popular extremes:

* "Dreams mean nothing—ignore them."

* "Dreams are messages—decode them."

Early Buddhist night practice supports a third position: **dreams reveal mind**, and the point is not decoding symbols but seeing construction, how emotion becomes narrative, how memory becomes present tense, how identity becomes believable with almost no evidence.

This is directly applicable to modern life because the same process runs during the day:

* the mind constructs stories,

* identifies with them,

* suffers as if they are fixed.

Seeing the process at night—when it is stripped down and exposed—can help a reader recognize it in waking life.

5) The chapter's role in the book's arc

Structurally, Chapter Ten bridges the earlier focus on dream portents and symbolic dreams to the more psychologically refined territory ahead. It shows that Buddhism's interest in dreams is not an isolated fascination—it belongs to a larger project: understanding the mind's fabrications and loosening identification with them.

In short: Chapter Ten is not saying "become a lucid dreamer."

It is saying something more radical: **the mind is trainable even at the edge of sleep**, and understanding does not have to stop when the lights go out.

CHAPTER ELEVEN — THE QUIET BEFORE THE LAST JOURNEY

Dawn rested lightly on the outskirts of Vesālī. Mist lifted from the rice paddies in slow, unhurried breaths, as though the land itself were waking from a long, quiet dream. Palm trees held their shadows close to their trunks. The sky was pale blue, not bright, only beginning.

The Buddha stood at the edge of the grove where the rains had passed. His robe hung loosely, the body thinner now, carrying the honest weight of age. Yet his presence was undiminished, not hardened, not heroic, only clear.

Nearby, monks gathered bowls, rolled mats, tightened straps over shoulders.

A departure, ordinary in shape.

And still, something in the air felt tender, as if the world had learned to speak more softly.

Later, the tradition would remember these days through the *Mahāparinibbāna Sutta*, not as a dream sequence, but as a turning so vast that even ordinary perception seemed to thin.[1]

The Canon does not say, *The Buddha had a final dream.* It says something quieter: the world trembled; the grove bloomed out of season; beings gathered from realms the eye does not usually see.[2]

Not as entertainment.

Not as proof.

As atmosphere, the way a room feels when a great presence is about to leave it.

The Buddha turned from the grove.

He began to walk.

The monks followed.

∼

The road took them past fields brightening under morning light, past wells and huts, past the small architecture of human life. Dust rose behind sandals. Birds cut the sky in simple arcs. A child called out to a mother across a path.

Everything unfolded as it always had, and yet the mind, standing close to endings, notices differently.

A single leaf fell.

It turned twice, caught light, then settled into earth.

For most, such moments pass unseen. But in this season of the story, impermanence seemed to announce itself in the smallest things not as philosophy, but as texture.

The Buddha walked on.

∼

Near Beluva, the sickness came.[3]

Not gently. The texts do not soften it. They do not make it symbolic. They describe pain, sharp and heavy, a body doing what bodies do. The monks watched for any sign that the Teacher would resist reality, that he would tighten against the fact of weakness. But nothing in him tightened. No quarrel with conditions. No inward narrative of injustice. Only the clear knowing that the body is conditioned, and therefore must change.

He continued teaching when he could, not from force, but from the same steady current that had carried him since Bodh Gaya: compassion without clinging.

He did not pretend the body was endless. He did not pretend his presence could be held.

He walked as far as he could walk. He rested when he needed to rest. He spoke when speech was useful. Then he grew silent again.

The monks followed in a widening ring of careful attention.

That night, beneath a high moon, the Buddha sat under a tree.

The grove was still. Not dead-still, alive-still—wind moving through leaves with the softness of breath.

The Canon records a great weariness in him, a fatigue like the unwinding of long threads.[4]

Yet alongside this weariness there was another quality, not grim endurance, but a settled resolve, as if he had already accepted what the body could not avoid.

No dream arose.

No visions arrived to console the mind. Because the liberated mind does not need consolation. It needs only to see.

The moonlight spread across the earth like pale cloth. And the night moved on.

In the days that followed, a subtle change entered the tone of his guidance. Not urgency as panic, but urgency as intimacy.

A tightening of the essential.

A distilling.

A turning of the disciple's gaze back toward the only refuge that does not depend on a single body: the Dhamma, and the training that makes the Dhamma real.

He spoke of diligence.

He spoke of impermanence.

He spoke as one preparing others to stand without leaning on him.

The road continued toward Pāvā, then beyond.

Toward Kusinārā.

The Portents at Kusinārā

The path grew long and uneven. Heat shimmered above fields.

The Buddha walked slowly now.

At times, stronger monks supported him. Not because he clung to strength. Because bodies have limits. And limits do not shame the liberated mind.

Somewhere along the road, the earth trembled, a great earthquake, so unusual the monks asked what could cause it.[5] The Buddha answered with the calm precision that never sought spectacle: such quaking can occur at great thresholds—when a Tathāgata is about to pass into final nibbāna.[6]

To the monks, the tremor was not merely ground. It was a shiver in the story of the world, a way of sensing, with the body, what the mind struggled to hold: the end was near.

They reached the outskirts of Kusinārā as day began to dim. The path entered a sal grove—pale trunks rising like pillars in soft evening light. This was the Upavattana of the Mallas.

The monks spread robes between twin sal trees. A bed for a weakened body.

The Canon says simply: the Buddha lay down on his right side, mindful and fully aware.[7] No drama in the movement. No last-minute mythology of resistance. Just the lion posture—steady, human, complete.

Then the grove did something strange. The sal trees bloomed out of season.[8] Blossoms fell like gentle rain over his body. White petals spiraled through the air as if the forest itself were offering a final homage.

It is the kind of scene that feels like a waking dream, not because it is unreal, but because meaning seems to have become visible for a moment in the shape of things.

The Buddha did not claim it.

He did not point to it as proof.

He let it fall.

He let it pass.

As night deepened, a stillness gathered in the grove.

Birds grew quiet.

Even small animals seemed to move with careful restraint, as if the forest were listening.

Then the Canon records another event plainly: beings from unseen realms assembled—devas and Brahmās gathering in vigil.[9] Some, it says, grieved. Some honored. Some stood in silent reverence.

To a mind untrained, this would feel like the atmosphere of dreams, where the invisible moves close.

But the sutta does not linger. It records. Then returns to what matters: the teaching.

The Buddha spoke not to dazzle, but to remind.

Not to reveal new doctrine, but to compress the old into its final clarity: everything conditioned passes. Be diligent. Rely on the Dhamma. Do not build your refuge out of what must change.[10]

The monks breathed softly.

Blossoms continued to fall.

A world was preparing to let go.

∾

Ānanda stood nearby, his heart trembling. For years he had been closest to the Teacher: attendant, listener, keeper of words. Now he faced the mind's unbearable doubling: the Buddha is here, and soon he will not be.

Ānanda wept and stepped aside, overwhelmed.[11]

The Buddha sent for him and spoke gently, not with denial, but with truth. Do not grieve as though something conditioned could be kept. What is born must pass. What is formed must dissolve.

This was not coldness. It was compassion without illusion. It was the mercy of a mind refusing to let another mind drown in the dream of permanence.

Ānanda bowed.

The grove held its breath.

The Dreaming Mind

The Last Question

A wanderer named Subhadda arrived late—uncertain, full of questions. The monks tried to turn him away. But the Buddha allowed him to enter.

Even now. Even at the end.

Subhadda asked what his heart needed to ask.

The Buddha answered with the same clear measure he had used all his life: where the Noble Eightfold Path is found, there awakening is found; where it is not, it is not.[12]

No ornament.

No seduction.

A compass.

A final refusal to let the mind substitute mystery for training.

Subhadda received the teaching. The story remembers him as the last disciple to be ordained by the Buddha.[13]

Then the grove returned to its quiet watch.

The Entering of Final Nibbāna

Between the twin sal trees, the Buddha lay. The body weakened. The mind remained undisturbed. This is the silent miracle the Canon insists upon: not that the body escaped death, but that awareness did not fall into confusion. The Buddha entered the meditative absorptions, the four jhānas, then moved through the formless attainments, as one who knows the terrain of mind as clearly as a traveler knows roads.[14]

He did not slip.

He did not drift.

He did not dream.

He met the ending with mastery, not mastery as control, but mastery as freedom from grasping.

Breath thinned.

Paused.

Returned.

Then grew faint again.

At last, the movement stilled.

And the sutta states it with a simplicity almost unbearable: the Blessed One attained final nibbāna.[15]

No trumpet.

No thunder.

No last vision painted across the mind.

Only release.

Complete.

Without remainder.

For those watching, the world felt unreal—not because it was false, but because the heart cannot easily take in a loss this clean.

Time softened.

Sound narrowed.

The grove seemed to hold a silence that was not empty but absolute.

Like the moment a long dream ends and the mind wakes holding air.

The monks bowed.

Some wept.

Some sat motionless, unable to name what rose in them.

Blossoms continued to fall for a while longer, as though the forest had not yet learned he was already gone.

After the Flame

In the hours that followed, the Mallas came to pay homage.[16]

Grief moved through the grove like heavy weather. Rites were prepared. The body was honored. The community began the ancient work of shaping memory into continuity.

But beneath the rites another truth remained: the Buddha had not left them a person to cling to. He had left them a path.

A way of seeing that does not depend on seasons or blossoms, on tremors or celestial witnesses.

A way of waking up even when the world is breaking.

The sal blossoms eventually stopped.

The grove returned to ordinary time.

Monks rose, wiped their faces, breathed again.

The world entered a new dawn without the Buddha's body, but not without the clarity he uncovered.

The dream of permanence had ended.

The discipline of seeing remained.

ANALYSIS: DREAMLIKE REALITY AND THE NATURE OF EXPERIENCE

Having established that dreams play an important narrative, ethical, and soteriological role in Buddhist traditions, the discussion here turns from *what dreams signify* to *what dreams reveal about reality itself*. The chapter demonstrates that dreams are not merely symbolic or prophetic phenomena within Buddhism, but function as one of its most powerful philosophical tools for interrogating perception, identity, and the apparent solidity of the world.

Across early Buddhist, Mahāyāna, and Yogācāra traditions, dreams are repeatedly invoked as a simile for lived experience. This is not incidental or decorative. Rather, the dream simile is employed because it captures a fundamental Buddhist insight: that what we ordinarily take to be stable, enduring, and intrinsically real is, in fact, conditioned, constructed, and dependent on cognitive processes. In this sense, the dream becomes an experiential analogue for ignorance (*avidyā*) itself.

Dreams as a Didactic Simile in Early Buddhism

In early Buddhist thought, particularly within Sthaviravāda traditions, dreams serve to illustrate the impermanent, insubstantial nature of the five aggregates (*pañcakkhandha*). The Buddha's use of similes—foam, bubbles, mirages, magical illusions, and dreams—aims to destabilize the intuitive belief in a solid self and a reliable external world. Among these, the dream simile is uniquely effective because it mirrors waking cognition so closely while remaining obviously illusory upon awakening.

The chapter shows that, for early Buddhism, the illusion does not lie in the existence of phenomena themselves, but in the *misapprehension* of their nature. Just as a dream is experienced vividly yet lacks enduring substance, so too do the aggregates arise and pass away without an underlying essence. Enlightenment (*bodhi*), in this framework, is not the destruction of experience, but the cessation of misperception. To awaken is, quite literally, to wake up from a dreamlike misunderstanding of reality.

This framing preserves ethical seriousness while undermining metaphysical reification. The world is not dismissed as meaningless; rather, it is understood as contingent and conditioned. This nuance becomes increasingly important as later Buddhist traditions deepen the philosophical implications of dreamlike existence.

The Dreaming Mind

. . .

Mahāyāna Radicalization: Emptiness and the Collapse of Ontological Certainty

Mahāyāna Buddhism intensifies the dream analogy by extending it beyond psychological misperception into a full ontological critique. In the *Prajñāpāramitā* literature and its Madhyamaka interpretation, all phenomena (*dharmas*), including the fundamental constituents posited by earlier Abhidharma systems, are declared empty (*śūnya*) of inherent existence (*svabhāva*).

Here, dreams no longer merely illustrate impermanence or selflessness; they exemplify the absence of intrinsic being altogether. A dream appears, functions, and disappears without ever having existed in the way it seemed to. Likewise, all phenomena arise dependently and are intelligible only within relational frameworks. Nāgārjuna's analysis dismantles the conceptual structures that support belief in stable existence, demonstrating that notions such as cause and effect, existence and non-existence, subject and object, have meaning only in relation to one another.

The chapter rightly emphasizes that this is not a form of nihilism. The dream simile does not deny experience but reframes it. Just as suffering within a dream feels real while dreaming, suffering in the conventional world is experientially valid and ethically significant. However, upon awakening, its ultimate status is revealed as empty of permanence and independent essence.

This insight leads to one of Mahāyāna's most distinctive claims: that liberation does not require escape from the world, but a transformation in how the world is understood. The realization that *saṃsāra* and *nirvāṇa* are not ultimately distinct rests precisely on this dreamlike ontology.

Yogācāra and the Dream as Cognitive Construction

The Yogācāra school pushes the dream analogy further still by examining the mechanics of perception itself. According to Yogācāra, waking experience and dreaming are structurally similar insofar as both are products of consciousness shaped by latent impressions (*vāsanā*) stored in the *ālaya-vijñāna*, or storehouse consciousness.

This perspective reframes reality as a cognitive event rather than a passive reception of external objects. Just as dream images arise without external stimuli, waking perceptions are likewise mediated by deeply ingrained mental patterns. The world appears coherent not because it exists independently in that form, but because multiple streams of consciousness share karmically conditioned structures.

The chapter highlights how Yogācāra philosophers respond to critiques regarding intersubjectivity and causal efficacy by pointing out that dreams themselves can produce real effects—fear, desire, bodily reactions—despite their illusory status. This further blurs the distinction between "real" and "unreal," shifting the focus from ontological substance to experiential consequence.

In doing so, Yogācāra provides a sophisticated psychological framework that anticipates many insights of modern cognitive science, particularly regarding perception as an active, constructive process.

Relevance for the Modern Reader

One of the chapter's most significant contributions lies in its relevance beyond historical or doctrinal analysis. The Buddhist use of dreams as a model for understanding reality resonates strongly with contemporary concerns about identity, perception, and mental health.

Modern psychology increasingly recognizes that human experience is shaped not by objective reality alone, but by interpretation, memory, expectation, and emotional conditioning. Anxiety, depression, and trauma often function much like dreams: internally generated narratives experienced as unquestionably real while occurring. The Buddhist dream analogy offers a way to relate to these experiences without denying their impact or becoming fully identified with them.

For contemporary readers, the idea that life is "like a dream" does not suggest escapism or detachment from responsibility. Instead, it provides a framework for cultivating flexibility, compassion, and discernment. Recognizing the constructed nature of experience allows individuals to respond rather than react, to question habitual assumptions, and to soften rigid self-concepts.

Furthermore, in an era shaped by digital realities, virtual identities, and mediated perception, the dream simile feels strikingly current. Online environments often generate emotional responses indistinguishable from those arising in physical contexts, reinforcing the Buddhist insight that perceived reality is deeply entangled with mental projection.

From a contemplative standpoint, this chapter also lays the philosophical groundwork for later discussions of Dream Yoga. If waking life itself is dreamlike, then learning to recognize and work skillfully with dreams becomes not an esoteric pursuit, but a training ground for awakening within everyday experience.

Integrative Significance within the Work

Within the structure of the overall work, this chapter functions as a conceptual hinge. It connects narrative and doctrinal discussions of dreams with practical applications in meditative and yogic traditions. By demonstrating that dreams are not marginal phenomena but central metaphors for understanding consciousness, the chapter justifies the later focus on Dream and Sleep Yoga as legitimate and meaningful Buddhist practices.

In doing so, it reinforces a core Buddhist message: awakening is not achieved by escaping experience, but by seeing clearly how experience arises. Dreams, far from being distractions, become mirrors—revealing both the fragility of perceived reality and the profound potential for liberation through understanding.

CHAPTER TWELVE — DREAMING IN THE MODERN WORLD

Night settles differently now.

It gathers not around silent forests or oil lamps trembling in the dark, but around apartment windows glowing blue with unfinished messages, around bedside tables cluttered with devices that never fully sleep, around minds still moving long after the body has grown tired.

A woman lies awake in a quiet room.

Outside, traffic hums—steady, distant, like a tide that never recedes.

Inside, her thoughts circle the day just passed: words spoken too quickly, silences misunderstood, tasks completed yet somehow unfinished.

When sleep finally comes, it arrives without ceremony.

The body loosens.

The mind releases its grip.

And dreams rise swiftly, not summoned, not chosen, but waiting just beyond the threshold.

The Dreaming Mind

She stands in a crowded street, searching for someone she cannot name. Buildings stretch at impossible angles. Voices echo without bodies.

A quiet unease settles in her chest, not fear exactly, but the feeling of being lost in a place that should be familiar.

She wakes with a soft gasp.

The room is unchanged.

The walls are solid.

The clock glows steadily beside the bed.

And yet something lingers—a sense that the dream has lifted a corner of the world she thought she understood.

She sits up, presses her palms together, and whispers into the dark:

What is this mind that dreams?

And what is this mind that wakes?

She does not know that centuries ago, in a world without electricity or clocks, a monk asked the Buddha almost the same question.

The Mind That Dreams Is the Mind That Wakes

Early Buddhism does not treat dreaming as a detour from reality, but as a window into its construction.

The dreamer in the modern apartment, the monk beneath a grove of trees, the traveler resting beside a fire—all move within the same architecture of mind.

In dreams, a world appears. A self appears. Emotion shapes experience instantly. Meaning forms without hesitation.

And when the dream ends, everything dissolves.

The Buddha asked something simple and radical:

Is waking life truly different?

When we open our eyes, the mind continues its work, organizing impressions, projecting meaning, clinging to what pleases, resisting what unsettles.

The difference is not *what* the mind does, but how invisible the process becomes.

Dreams reveal, with startling clarity, that experience is built, moment by moment, from perception, memory, emotion, and habit.

In waking life, the same construction continues, but we forget we are building anything at all. This is why the Buddha taught that "the world" arises with perception and ceases when perception ceases.[1] Dreams are not interruptions to life. They are mirrors—showing how the mind operates continuously.

∼

Illusion Seen Up Close

When the woman wakes unsettled, she encounters a truth the early texts make explicit: The mind creates convincing worlds with astonishing ease.

In dreams, fear becomes danger, desire becomes fulfillment, confusion reshapes landscapes, identity shifts without resistance.

Waking life follows the same pattern.

Stories arise—about who we are, about who others are, about success and failure, about what the future holds and what the past has already ruined.

We believe these stories with the same certainty a dreamer believes a dream.

Dreams do not deceive us. They reveal how easily we are deceived.

They show, compressed and undeniable, how swiftly the mind builds a world and how quickly that world collapses when conditions change.

Seeing this, something loosens. The grip around daily narratives softens. Certainty gives way to curiosity.

The world remains, but it no longer feels quite so solid.

Dreams as Teachers in a Secular Age

The Buddha did not encourage symbol-hunting or prophecy. He encouraged understanding.

In a modern world saturated with noise, dreams remain one of the few spaces where the mind speaks honestly.

A dream of falling reveals instability. A dream of being chased reveals unresolved fear. A dream of losing someone reveals grief that had no words.

Not because dreams are mystical, but because the mind relaxes its guard.

What is hidden by daylight rises at night.

In this way, dreams become teachers, not of fate, but of pattern.

They show where the heart is knotted, where attention is stuck, where the story of "me" has hardened into habit.

And sometimes, quietly, they show a longing for freedom.

The Dreamlike Texture of Waking Life

Morning comes.

Light slips through the blinds.

Dust drifts slowly in the air.

The woman sits on the edge of her bed, watching her breath as the city wakes around her.

A question lingers: *What if the dream wasn't meaningless?*

What if it revealed how my waking mind behaves every day? This question stands at the threshold of the Buddha's teaching. The Buddha did not claim that life is a dream. He claimed that experience is conditioned: shaped by perception, colored by emotion, filtered through habit.

Dreams show this process nakedly.

In waking life, it happens more slowly, and so we rarely notice. But the mechanism is the same. When this is seen, the world does not disappear. It becomes workable. The stories lose their tyranny. The self loosens its grip. Experience opens.

A Small Lucidity

That evening, the woman sits quietly with a cup of tea.

She remembers the dream again, not to analyze it, but to observe it. She notices how fear shaped the world. How quickly meaning formed. How real it all felt until the moment of waking.

And then, a small lucidity.

If the mind can create worlds at night, it must be shaping her days as well.

Not magically.

Not metaphorically.

But mechanically.

She does not feel frightened.

She feels awake.

Not awakened, but slightly more spacious.

The Buddha called this *yoniso manasikāra*: wise attention. The mind turning toward clarity instead of habit.

It changes nothing immediately. And yet, it changes everything.

Dreaming Toward Awakening

Night returns.

She lies down again, not waiting for dreams, not fearing them, not trying to control them. She simply rests.

A thought passes gently through the mind: *What might I see tonight?*

Not as demand.

Not as hope.

As openness.

She closes her eyes.

And this willingness to meet experience without resistance is already a kind of waking.

The mind that dreams at night is the same mind that builds the world by day.

To see one clearly is to begin seeing the other.

This is the doorway left open by the ancient teachings.

A doorway still waiting in modern rooms, beneath modern skies, inside modern lives.

The dream continues.

And so does the possibility of waking.

ANALYSIS: DREAMS, MENTAL CONSTRUCTION, AND MODERN RELEVANCE

Chapter Twelve completes the arc of the book by bringing Buddhist dream theory decisively into the present. Where earlier chapters explored dreams as omens, symbols, and contemplative phenomena within ancient Buddhist contexts, this chapter demonstrates that the core insight underlying those traditions remains directly applicable to modern life.

Building on the framework established earlier in the book, this chapter brings dream-theory into the modern world—showing how the same mechanisms of construction operate under screens, stress, and overstimulation.

For modern readers—especially those shaped by psychological and cognitive frameworks—this insight is immediately recognizable. Contemporary neuroscience confirms that perception is not passive reception but active construction. Buddhism articulated this experiential truth long before modern science provided its models.

The chapter's relevance lies in its ethical and practical implications. If suffering arises largely from the mind's unexamined stories, then insight does not require withdrawal from life but clarity within it. Dreams offer a nightly rehearsal of this insight, showing how quickly fear, desire, and identity fabricate entire worlds.

Importantly, the chapter avoids romanticizing dreams or advocating esoteric practice. Instead, it frames dream-awareness as a gateway to *lucid living*: the capacity to notice when perception hardens into belief and emotion masquerades as truth. This is the foundation of mindfulness itself.

In this way, Chapter Twelve reframes dreams not as curiosities of sleep but as teachers of waking life. The book concludes not with doctrine, but with invitation—an invitation to see clearly how experience is made, and how it may, with patience and attention, be gently unmade.

CONCLUSION: THE QUIET WHERE DREAM AND DAWN MEET

Night softens.

Not in the dramatic way evening spills color across the sky, but in the quieter way darkness loosens, as though it, too, has been holding its breath.

Somewhere, a person lies half awake. The mind rests on that fragile seam where images drift without command and thoughts move gently, as if unsure whether to form or fade.

This is where dreams rise. Where memory stretches its hand. Where fear whispers beneath the surface. Where longing shows its shadowed shape.

Even the dreams we forget leave traces in the body, a faint mood, a shift of breath, a question held somewhere behind the ribs.

The Buddha said the world is known through the mind, arising with perception, ceasing when perception ceases.[1] Perhaps this is why so much of what matters first appears in the quiet before morning.

This book began in such a place.

And now, after following the dreams of queens, monks, wanderers, and an awakening sage, we return here, to the threshold where understanding begins to open.

∼

What This Journey Revealed

Across these chapters, dreams were never merely decoration.

They functioned as doorways into the interior life of Buddhist thought, a way to watch the mind when it is least defended, and therefore most honest.

We began with a dream that carried the weight of an era: Queen Māyā's vision, tender and impossible, the world's future arriving first as an image in sleep.

We followed Asita's recognition, that strange mixture of awe and grief that sometimes arises when one sees clearly: joy for what is coming, sadness for what one will not live to receive.

We listened to Yaśodharā's five visions as they revealed the human cost of awakening, how the path is never only philosophical, never only personal, but relational, disruptive, real.

We moved through Siddhārtha's dreams before renunciation, those internal tremors that foreshadow the moment a life can no longer remain the same life.

We witnessed the Buddha-to-be at the edge of awakening, when the mind grows luminous and pliable, and the world's seeming solidity begins to thin.

We then entered the dreams of monks and practitioners, not as prophecy-hunters, but as people learning to see: learning how fear becomes landscape, how desire becomes narrative, how identity becomes a role believed too quickly.

We walked through meditative states where perception becomes dreamlike, not because reality is false, but because the mind's construction of reality is finally seen up close.

And then, at last, we stepped into the modern room: screens glowing, minds overstimulated, sleep arriving late and scattered, and asked the question that quietly underlies every chapter: *What does the dream reveal about the mind that lives my life?*

Dreams, it turns out, are not interruptions of consciousness.

They are expressions of it—unfiltered, unedited, often more truthful than waking thought permits.

They reveal how memory reshapes itself, how fear repeats, how longing disguises itself, how the sense of "I" is assembled moment by moment, and how the mind continues its quiet work long after the world has gone to sleep.

∽

What Early Buddhism Actually Teaches About Dreams

Early Buddhism treats dreams as conditioned experiences—neither oracles to worship nor noise to ignore.

The commentarial tradition also preserves a practical framework for causation in dreams, which I have already outlined earlier in the book. Here, it matters for one reason: it keeps us balanced—neither romanticizing dreams nor dismissing them.[2] Not every dream is significant, and not every dream is meaningless. They are mind *events* shaped by habit, perception, memory, and karma. To understand dreams, then, is not to become a collector of symbols. It is to become intimate with the mind that produces experience.

∽

What Dreams Teach About Waking Reality

A central thread has run beneath every chapter: experience is not passively received—it is *conditioned*, interpreted, and continually shaped.

In early Buddhist analysis, experience arises through conditions: contact, perception, feeling, intention, consciousness, and the chain of dependent arising that follows.³ Moment by moment, the world is known, interpreted, reacted to, re-made. Dreams reveal this construction with unmistakable clarity.

In dreams you can see:

* how quickly a world forms

* how real it feels

* how emotion shapes perception

* how identity shifts without resistance

* how suffering arises without external cause

* how relief appears simply by waking

To understand dreaming is to recognize something humbling: The mind can create an entire world in sleep, and suffer inside it, without anyone else participating.

Waking life, of course, contains external conditions. But the *texture* of suffering often arises from the mind's overlay:

* stories added to events

* assumptions added to uncertainty

* identity added to feeling

* permanence added to what is changing

A dream does not distort the world. It exposes how much distortion

is already present. And in that exposure lies the possibility of freedom:

If a nightmare dissolves when you wake, perhaps suffering dissolves when the mind wakes to its own habits.

Awakening, in this sense, is not the end of dreaming. It is the end of being lost in what the mind creates.

As proposed earlier in this book (as an interpretive lens rather than doctrine), some prophetic dreams may be read as the mind intuiting karmic conditions approaching ripening; their value lies less in prediction than in what they reveal about the conditioned patterning of experience.

∼

Why Dreams Still Matter in Modern Life

You live in a world that forgets the night.

Screens glow past midnight. Tasks spill across hours. Many people move through their days too hurried to notice the quieter movements of the mind.

But every night, independent of your intention, the mind performs its ancient work:

* reorganizing memory

* softening emotional knots

* surfacing unspoken fears

* revealing patterns

* loosening tension

* hinting at what is unresolved

* and sometimes—rarely—showing what is approaching

Dreams are not random noise. They are a conversation, the mind speaking to itself in its own language.

Modern psychology, from its own angle, has begun to confirm what Buddhism saw long ago: dreams reveal how experience is constructed, how the sense of self is shaped, how fear repeats, how desire moves, how memory rearranges itself each time it is touched. And occasionally, dreams show what the waking mind is not yet ready to acknowledge.

This is why dreams remain relevant: they reflect the truth you carry before you have words for it.

∼

Humanity's Long Companionship With Dreams

Across cultures and centuries, human beings have turned toward dreams to understand what waking life cannot easily reveal.

Dream temples and incubation rituals. Indigenous vision practices. Buddhist narratives and contemplative disciplines. Each tradition recognized that dreams carry a different kind of truth. Not always literal. Not always symbolic. But meaningful in the way they bring us closer to the movements of our own hearts. This book takes its place within that long human conversation, offering not final answers, but a clearer way to sit with the questions.

∼

A Final Practice: How to Hold Your Dreams Lightly

If you have read this far, you already know that dreams are not interruptions; they are invitations.

You do not need to interpret every symbol or solve every image like a puzzle. Instead, you can practice something simpler:

* Notice how the dream *felt*

* Notice what it revealed about fear, longing, habit

* Notice what story the mind was eager to believe

* Notice what identity it tried to protect

* Notice where the heart tightened

* Notice where the heart softened

Sometimes a dream points to what you have avoided.

Sometimes it reflects what you already know.

Sometimes it shows the turning of karma.

And sometimes—rarely—it offers a glimpse of something gathering at the edge of your life.

Dreams do not guarantee certainty. But they offer a kind of truth, the quiet kind that waits patiently for you to listen.

Night begins to lighten.

The person who lay drifting moves gently, a shoulder shifting, a breath deepening. A dream fades in the space behind the eyes.

Morning enters the room softly, without urgency.

The person wakes.

They may not remember the dream, but something inside them is slightly different, a softened edge, a small clarity in how thought forms.

This is how awakening begins: not with thunder, not with revelation, but with a quiet recognition that the mind is deeper and more fluid than you ever knew.

The Buddha woke beneath a tree two and a half millennia ago.

You wake in your own room now.

Both awakenings begin the same way, with the mind starting to see what it has always been shaping.

Dreams are not the destination. They are the whisper before the turning. A reminder that waking reality, too, is conditioned. A reminder that clarity is possible. A reminder that freedom begins quietly in the places you once overlooked.

And in the soft moment after a dream dissolves, you may feel what he felt: a mind beginning to wake.

A NOTE TO THE READER

If something in these pages stayed with you —

a dream,

a question,

a quiet shift in how you notice your inner world —

then the book has done what it was meant to do.

If you feel moved to share a few words about your experience, an honest review—wherever you purchased the book—helps this work find its way to other readers who may be carrying similar questions.

Thank you for reading, and for taking this journey into the quiet places of the mind.

APPENDIX A: DREAM EPISODES IN THE PĀLI CANON

A Complete List of Dream Passages in Early Buddhist Texts

This appendix gathers all identifiable dream episodes in the Pāli Canon.

Only canonical sources are included.

Organized for clarity, with full references.

I. Prophetic or Significant Dreams

1. The Bodhisatta's Five Great Dreams

Dīgha Nikāya 14 (Mahāpadāna Sutta)

Before his awakening, the Bodhisatta experienced five dreams foretelling his enlightenment. The Buddha later recounts these dreams to his disciples.

2. King Pasenadi's Dream of Burning Embers

Saṃyutta Nikāya 3.25 (Piyajātika Sutta)

King Pasenadi dreams of seven glowing embers. The Buddha interprets them as symbols of attachment and anger arising among those in the king's court.

3. King Pasenadi's Four Dreams
Aṅguttara Nikāya 4.115 (Pāṭikaṅga Sutta)

Four troubling dreams are brought to the Buddha. He offers grounded interpretations that point to political and social decline rather than supernatural omens.

4. Cowherd Nanda's Dream of Cows Crossing Water
Saṃyutta Nikāya 35.197

Nanda dreams of cows crossing a river. The Buddha uses this as a teaching on how beings cross from confusion to clarity through right view.

II. Dreams Referenced as Unreliable or Misleading
5. Dreams Among "Empty Signs" Leading to Delusion
Majjhima Nikāya 2 (Sabbāsava Sutta)

Dreams are included among mental images that, when taken as literal messages, increase delusion and reinforce unskillful speculation.

6. False Claims Based on Dreams or Visions
Majjhima Nikāya 12 (Mahāsīhanāda Sutta)

The Buddha criticizes ascetics who falsely claim spiritual attainments based on dreams or unclear visions.

III. Dreams as Natural Mental Phenomena

7. Dreams Arising from "What One Frequently Thinks About"

Saṃyutta Nikāya 1.20 (Paṭhamasupina Sutta)

A verse teaching that dreams arise from daily mental preoccupation — what the mind repeatedly dwells upon.

8. Dreams Used as Analogies for Impermanence and Appearance

(These are metaphorical references, not literal dreams.)

- **Saṃyutta Nikāya 22.95 (Phena Sutta)** — perceptual experience compared to a dream, mirage, bubble, foam.
- **Dhammapada 170** — the world seen like a dream by those who look clearly.
- **Theragāthā 19.1** — fleeting mental images likened to dream imagery.

These passages illuminate the constructed nature of experience.

IV. Dreams in the Vinaya (Monastic Code)

9. Sexual Dreams and Monastic Rules

Vinaya, Pācittiya 45

A monk who experiences a sexual dream incurs *no offense*, acknowledging dreams as involuntary mental events.

10. Dreams and Purity of Conduct

Vinaya, Mahāvagga I.6

Clarifications that dreams do not constitute breaches of celibacy or vows.

V. Commentarial Interpretations with Canonical Parallels

11. Later Commentarial Attributions Regarding Dreams

In later Buddhist tradition, dreams are sometimes explained through a set of commonly cited causes, including:

1. Bodily conditions

2. Past impressions

3. Mental preoccupation

4. Influence of devas

5. Prophetic dreams

These explanatory categories reflect broader Buddhist themes concerning kamma, perception (saññā), and mental conditioning, but do not appear as a unified list in the early Nikāyas or in a clearly identifiable passage of the *Visuddhimagga*.

VI. Common Dreams *Not* Found in the Pāli Canon

To avoid confusion, here are well-known Buddhist dream narratives **not present in the Pāli Canon:**

- Queen Māyā's conception dream
- Yaśodharā's five dreams
- The Bodhisatta's dream before renunciation
- The dream predicting enlightenment
- The dream of a mountain of dung

These appear in **later Sanskrit and Mahāyāna texts**, especially the *Lalitavistara Sūtra*, not in Theravāda sources.

APPENDIX B: DREAM SYMBOLISM IN EARLY BUDDHIST SOURCES

Dreams in early Buddhism are interpreted differently from those in later Sanskrit and Tibetan traditions.

Where later traditions often focus on rich symbolic imagery, early Pāli sources emphasize **function**, **cause**, and **mental conditioning** rather than symbolic decoding.

This appendix gathers the few symbolic elements that *do* appear in early Buddhism, along with their canonical or commentarial grounding.

I. Symbolism in the Bodhisatta's Five Great Dreams

(DN 14)

1. Lying with the head to the Himalayas

Represents the future Buddha's influence spreading across the world.

2. Grass growing from his navel to the sky

Symbol of teachings that "reach far" and nourish many beings.

3. White worms covering his body to the knees

Often interpreted as future disciples or followers.

4. Birds of many colours settling on his body, becoming white

Symbolizes diverse beings entering the path and becoming purified.

5. Walking on fifth that rose to his ankles

Represents the burden of teaching the world — the "dust of beings" he must guide.

These are **canonical** symbolic dreams — the strongest in early Buddhism.

II. Symbolism in King Pasenadi's Dreams

1. Seven embers (SN 3.25)

Unresolved anger in the royal court.

2. Four dream-omens (AN 4.115)

Not omens in a supernatural sense; the Buddha interprets them in psychological and social terms.

III. Symbolism in Commentaries (Non-Canonical)

(Used carefully and only where consistent with early teachings.)

From the *Visuddhimagga*:

1. Snakes → deception or anger

Reflecting mental states rather than objective events.

2. Falling → instability of ethical grounding

A psychological rather than supernatural reading.

3. Water → emotion or desire

Common symbolic motif borrowed from Indian interpretive traditions.

These are useful but should be read as **commentarial**, not canonical.

IV. Why Early Buddhism Avoids Heavy Symbolism

• The Buddha discouraged magical thinking based on dreams (MN 2, MN 12).

• He encouraged interpretations grounded in **causes and conditions**, not superstition.

• Dreams were to be understood through **psychology**, **ethics**, and **kamma**, not through external symbols.

The emphasis is always on:

• mental habit

• karmic tendencies

• emotional residue

• preoccupation

• bodily conditions

• spiritual insight

Rather than symbolism for its own sake.

V. When Symbolism *Does* Appear

Symbolism is used only when:

1 It supports a deeper ethical or spiritual point, or

2 The dream involves a Bodhisatta or spiritually advanced figure.

These symbolic dreams are rare and carefully framed to avoid superstition.

VI. Why This Matters for Modern Readers

Understanding early Buddhist symbolic logic helps avoid:

- over-interpretation
- external fortune-telling
- reliance on omens
- confusion between early and later traditions

It also restores a grounded, clear framework for dream practice that supports psychological maturity and spiritual insight.

APPENDIX C: COMPARISON OF DREAM NARRATIVES IN THE PĀLI CANON AND THE LALITAVISTARA SŪTRA

Dreams appear throughout Buddhist literature, but they are not treated uniformly.

The **Pāli Canon** presents dreams as rare, psychologically grounded insights arising from causes and conditions.

The **Lalitavistara Sūtra**, a later Sanskrit biography of the Buddha, presents dreams as richly symbolic narratives woven into a cosmic story.

This appendix clarifies the differences so readers can understand which dream episodes belong to early Buddhism and which belong to later traditions.

I. Dreams Found in the Pāli Canon but Rare or Absent in Later Sanskrit Texts

1 The Bodhisatta's Five Great Dreams

(DN 14 — Mahāpadāna Sutta)

These five dreams directly reference the Bodhisatta's impending awakening.

They are among the few dream narratives the Canon preserves with symbolic interpretation.

2 King Pasenadi's Dreams

(SN 3.25; AN 4.115)

The Buddha interprets the king's troubling dreams in ethical and social terms, not supernatural ones.

3 Cowherd Nanda's Dream

(SN 35.197)

Used as a teaching on right view and the crossing from confusion to clarity.

4 Dreams mentioned as unreliable or misleading

(MN 2; MN 12)

The Buddha cautions against taking dreams as omens or spiritual attainments.

5 Dreams as mental constructions

(SN 1.20; SN 22.95)

Dreams illustrate the conditioned nature of perception.

6 Dreams in the Vinaya

Sexual dreams are explicitly recognized as involuntary and non-offensive events.

(Pācittiya 45; Mahāvagga I.6)

These narratives form the core of **Theravāda dream discourse**.

II. Dreams Absent in the Pāli Canon but Prominent in the Lalitavistara Sūtra

The following dream episodes **do not appear** in the Pāli Canon but are well known because of the later Sanskrit tradition:

1 Queen Māyā's Conception Dream

A white elephant enters her womb.

This story is central to Buddhist art and ritual but **not** canonical in Pāli sources.

2 Dreams predicting the Bodhisatta's birth

Highly symbolic and cosmological.

3 Yaśodharā's dreams before Siddhārtha's renunciation

Five dreams foretelling his departure.

4 Siddhārtha's own dream before leaving the palace

A dark forest or path appears, offering symbolic instruction.

5 Dreams predicting enlightenment

Occur in various embellished biographies, but again, not in the Pāli Canon.

6 Dream of a mountain of dung

Often cited but absent from early sources; appears in later Sanskrit and commentarial literature.

The Lalitavistara's dream world is more **mythic, devotional, and dramatic**, designed to inspire awe.

III. Why These Traditions Differ

1. Tone and Purpose

- **Pāli Canon**: grounded, psychological, ethical; rooted in everyday causality.

- **Lalitavistara**: expansive, devotional, cosmological; emphasizing the Buddha as a universal figure.

2. Use of Symbolism

- **Pāli Canon**: sparse, carefully applied.
- **Lalitavistara**: lavish symbolic narratives such as elephants, jewels, palaces, deities.

3. Interpretation

- **Pāli Canon**: dreams explained through mind, karma, and conditions.
- **Lalitavistara**: dreams interpreted through cosmic storytelling and royal prophecy.

IV. Guidance for This Book

This book:

- draws philosophical grounding from the **Pāli Canon**,
- includes narrative material from the **Lalitavistara Sūtra** *only when clearly indicated*,
- and avoids merging the two traditions.

This appendix ensures clarity for scholars and general readers alike.

APPENDIX D: HOW TO WORK WITH DREAMS IN BUDDHIST PRACTICE

A Practical Guide for Modern Readers

Dreams are not supernatural messages nor meaningless noise.

They *are movements of your own mind*, revealing patterns, emotions, habits, and karmic tendencies that may be hidden during the day.

This appendix offers a practical way to relate to dreams without superstition or over-analysis.

∼

I. Beginning a Gentle Dream Practice

1. **Upon waking, stay still for a moment.**
Before thought returns fully, the mood of the dream can still be felt.

2. **Notice the emotional residue.**

Dreams speak through feeling more than imagery.

3. Record only what remains vivid.

A short note is enough; you are observing the mind, not creating a catalogue.

II. Understanding Dreams Through Early Buddhist Frameworks

Early Buddhism identifies **five causes** of dreams:

1. **Bodily conditions** — illness, stress, food, sleep quality.

2. **Past impression** — memory resurfacing.

3. **Mental preoccupation** — what occupied you during the day.

4. **Influence of other beings** — devas appearing through subtle mind-to-mind contact.

5. **Prophetic intuition** — dreams sensing karmic ripening.

Ask yourself which cause feels closest.

This brings curiosity and clarity, not dogmatic interpretation.

III. When a Dream Repeats

Repetition suggests:

- an unresolved story
- a persistent fear
- a longing needing acknowledgement

Sit with it gently.

Often the dream stops once the underlying emotion is seen clearly.

IV. When a Dream Feels Prophetic

Instead of treating it as prediction, ask:

* **"What karmic momentum might be approaching expression?"**

* **"What behaviours or tendencies is the dream showing me?"**

Prophetic dreams may be the mind sensing conditions already forming.

They are not to inspire fear, but insight.

V. A Simple Daily Dream Practice

Before sleep:

1. Sit quietly for a minute.

2. Let the mind soften.

3. Set a gentle intention:
"Let me understand my mind."

Upon waking:

4. Notice what feeling remains.

5. Hold it with kindness.

6. Reflect without forcing meaning.

∼

VI. Dreams in the Context of Meditation

Practitioners may encounter:

- light or colour

- floating sensations
- rising memories
- images from past experiences
- dissolving boundaries of identity

These are not signs of attainment.

They are signs of transparency—the mind showing itself without filters.

Treat them as the Buddha advised: with steadiness, clarity, and non-grasping.

~

VII. The Deepest Insight

Dreams reveal that:

- the mind constructs experience
- the mind believes its own constructions
- the mind suffers inside those constructions
- and the mind can wake from them

This is why dreams matter—they illustrate the Dhamma intimately.

~

VIII. A Closing Encouragement

Think of a dream that once stayed with you.

· · ·

Ask:

- What part of me spoke through that dream?
- What truth was rising?
- What longing or fear was being revealed?

Dreams are invitations, not puzzles to solve, but thresholds into more profound understanding.

GLOSSARY OF BUDDHIST TERMS

Aṅguttara Nikāya (AN)

One of the major collections of the Pāli Canon.

Organized by numbered lists, containing teachings on ethics, meditation, and the nature of mind.

Anicca

Impermanence.

The truth that all conditioned things arise, change, and pass away—in waking life and in dreams.

Anattā

Non-self.

The absence of a permanent, unchanging essence behind experience.

A key insight into why both dreams and waking perceptions feel real but are not fixed.

Āsava

GLOSSARY OF BUDDHIST TERMS

Mental "taints" or deep-rooted tendencies—including craving, ignorance, and attachment—that keep beings bound to suffering.

Āsavakkhayañāṇa

The "knowledge of the destruction of the taints."

The third watch of the Buddha's night of awakening, when liberation becomes complete.

Bhavaṅga

The "life-continuum" mind.

In later Theravāda thought, the stream of consciousness that flows when active mental processes rest—including during sleep.

Bodhisatta / Bodhisattva

A being on the path toward Buddhahood.

Used in Pāli texts for the Buddha in his previous lives and in his life before awakening.

Cutūpapātañāṇa

Knowledge of the passing away and reappearance of beings according to their actions.

The second watch of the Buddha's night of awakening, revealing the lawful relationship between intention (kamma) and rebirth.

Dhamma / Dharma

The teachings of the Buddha, the truth of reality, and the law of nature that governs experience.

Dukkha

Suffering, dissatisfaction, or unease—the fundamental tension that arises when the mind clings to what changes.

Jātaka

Stories of the Buddha's past lives.

Many include dream episodes that foreshadow moral lessons or future events.

Jhāna

Deep meditative absorption.

A state of profound stillness and clarity where the mind becomes unified.

Kamma / Karma

Intentional action that plants seeds for future experience.

Central to understanding how dreams may reflect tendencies or karmic conditions nearing ripening.

Khandha (Aggregates)

The five components of experience: form, feeling, perception, mental formations, and consciousness.

Together they create the sense of "I," both in dreams and waking life.

Lalitavistara Sūtra

A Sanskrit biography of the Buddha preserved in the Mahāyāna tradition.

Important for its dream narratives surrounding the Buddha's conception and early life.

Māra

The personification of delusion and obstruction.

Appears in dreams, temptations, and psychological struggles on the path to awakening.

Majjhima Nikāya (MN)

The "Middle-Length Discourses" of the Buddha—a key canonical source for teachings on meditation and the nature of mind.

Ñāṇa

Direct knowledge or insight.

In early Buddhism, a form of knowing that sees phenomena clearly and decisively, distinct from symbolic, conceptual, or intuitive cognition.

Nimitta

A mental "sign," often visual or luminous, that appears during meditation as concentration deepens.

Not directly related to prophetic dreaming, though sometimes confused with it.

Nirodha

Cessation.

The ending of suffering when craving falls away.

Pabhassara

"Luminous" or "radiant."

A term used in early Buddhist texts to describe the mind's natural clarity when defilements are absent or temporarily stilled; not equivalent to awakening.

Paṭiccasamuppāda

Dependent arising.

The truth that all phenomena—including dreams—arise because conditions support them, and cease when those conditions change.

Pīti

GLOSSARY OF BUDDHIST TERMS

Joy or rapture arising in meditation.

Sometimes appears in light dreams or dreams of flying.

Pāli Canon

The earliest complete collection of the Buddha's teachings preserved in the Theravāda tradition.

Pubbenivāsānussatiñāṇa

Knowledge of past lives—the first watch of the Buddha's awakening.

Saṃyutta Nikāya (SN)

A canonical collection organized by thematic groups—including teachings on perception, illusion, and the nature of mind.

Samsāra

The cycle of birth, death, and rebirth driven by craving and ignorance.

Satipaṭṭhāna

Foundations of mindfulness.

The practice of observing body, feeling, mind, and mental objects with clarity.

Sutta / Sūtra

Discourses of the Buddha.

"Sutta" is the Pāli term; "Sūtra" is Sanskrit.

Tathāgata

A title for the Buddha meaning "Thus-Gone" or "Thus-Come," referring to one who has awakened.

Vipassanā

GLOSSARY OF BUDDHIST TERMS

Insight meditation—seeing clearly the impermanent, conditioned, and non-self nature of all experience.

Visuddhimagga

A foundational 5th-century commentary by Buddhaghosa.

Provides early Buddhist explanations of the five causes of dreams.

NOTES

Epigraph

1. Bodhi, Bhikkhu, trans. *The Numerical Discourses of the Buddha: A Translation of the Aṅguttara Nikāya*. Boston: Wisdom Publications, 2012.

CHAPTER ONE — The Creature That Dreams

1. Rupert Gethin, *The Foundations of Buddhism* (Oxford: Oxford University Press, 1998), 112–18.
2. Bhikkhu Ñāṇamoli and Bhikkhu Bodhi, trans., *The Middle Length Discourses of the Buddha: A Translation of the Majjhima Nikāya* (Boston: Wisdom Publications, 1995), MN 1 (Mūlapariyāya Sutta) and MN 18 (Madhupiṇḍika Sutta).
3. Robert Stickgold and Matthew P. Walker, "Sleep-Dependent Memory Consolidation and Reconfiguration," *Journal of Sleep Research* 14, no. 3 (September 2005): 213–223, https://doi.org/10.1111/j.1365-2869.2005.00437.x.
4. Ñāṇamoli and Bodhi, *Middle Length Discourses*, MN 18.
5. Rupert Gethin, *The Foundations of Buddhism* (Oxford: Oxford University Press, 1998), 112–18.
6. Ñāṇamoli and Bodhi, *Middle Length Discourses*, MN 18.

CHAPTER TWO — The Dream That Began a World

1. Buddhaghosa, *The Path of Purification (Visuddhimagga)*, trans. Bhikkhu Ñāṇamoli (Kandy: Buddhist Publication Society, 2010), XII.55–57.
2. Bhikkhu Bodhi, trans., *The Sutta Nipāta: An Ancient Collection of the Buddha's Discourses Together with Its Commentaries* (Boston: Wisdom Publications, 2017), Sn 3.11.
3. Bodhi, Bhikkhu, trans. *The Numerical Discourses of the Buddha: A Translation of the Aṅguttara Nikāya*. Boston: Wisdom Publications, 2012, AN 3.25.
4. Bays, Gwendolyn, trans. *The Lalitavistara Sūtra: The Voice of the Buddha*. Berkeley: Dharma Publishing, 1983, 39–45.
5. Buddhaghosa, *The Path of Purification (Visuddhimagga)*, trans. Bhikkhu Ñāṇamoli (Kandy: Buddhist Publication Society, 2010), XII.55–57.
6. Bhikkhu Bodhi, trans., *The Sutta Nipāta: An Ancient Collection of the Buddha's Discourses Together with Its Commentaries* (Boston: Wisdom Publications, 2017), Sn 3.11.

Notes

CHAPTER THREE — Dreams in the Buddha's Early Life

1. Bays, Gwendolyn, trans. *The Lalitavistara Sūtra: The Voice of the Buddha*. Berkeley: Dharma Publishing, 1983, 51–55.
2. Ñāṇamoli, Bhikkhu, and Bhikkhu Bodhi, trans. *The Middle Length Discourses of the Buddha: A Translation of the Majjhima Nikāya*. Boston: Wisdom Publications, 1995, MN 36 (Mahāsaccaka Sutta); see also Buddhaghosa, *The Path of Purification (Visuddhimagga)*, trans. Bhikkhu Ñāṇamoli (Kandy: Buddhist Publication Society, 2010), 154–65.
3. Ñāṇamoli, Bhikkhu, and Bhikkhu Bodhi, trans. *The Middle Length Discourses of the Buddha: A Translation of the Majjhima Nikāya*. Boston: Wisdom Publications, 1995. MN 36 (Mahāsaccaka Sutta).
4. Ibid.
5. Walshe, Maurice, trans. *The Long Discourses of the Buddha: A Translation of the Dīgha Nikāya*. Boston: Wisdom Publications, 1995. DN 2 (Samaññaphala Sutta).
6. Cowell, E. B., ed. *The Jātaka or Stories of the Buddha's Former Births*. 6 vols. Cambridge: Cambridge University Press, 1895–1907.

CHAPTER FOUR — Dreams on the Eve of Renunciation

1. Gwendolyn Bays, trans., *The Lalitavistara Sūtra: The Voice of the Buddha* (Berkeley: Dharma Publishing, 1983), 183–188.
2. Ibid., 97–101.
3. John S. Strong, *The Buddha: A Short Biography* (Oxford: Oneworld Publications, 2001), 45–52.

CHAPTER FIVE — The Five Great Dreams

1. Bhikkhu Bodhi, trans., *The Numerical Discourses of the Buddha: A Translation of the Aṅguttara Nikāya* (Somerville, MA: Wisdom Publications, 2012), Aṅguttara Nikāya 5.196–197 (Mahāsupina Suttas).
2. Bhikkhu Bodhi, trans., *The Numerical Discourses of the Buddha: A Translation of the Aṅguttara Nikāya* (Somerville, MA: Wisdom Publications, 2012), Aṅguttara Nikāya 5.196–197 (Mahāsupina Suttas).

CHAPTER SIX — The Night the Mind Opened

1. Bhikkhu Ñāṇamoli and Bhikkhu Bodhi, trans., *The Middle Length Discourses of the Buddha: A Translation of the Majjhima Nikāya* (Boston: Wisdom Publications, 1995), MN 36 (Mahāsaccaka Sutta).
2. Thanissaro Bhikkhu, trans., "Bhaya-bherava Sutta: Fear and Terror (MN 4)," *Access to Insight*, accessed December 18, 2025, [https://www.accesstoinsight.org/tipitaka/mn/mn.004.than.html]
3. Ibid.

4. Ibid.
5. Nyanaponika Thera, trans., "Dhammacakkappavattana Sutta: Setting the Wheel of Dhamma in Motion (SN 56.11)," *Access to Insight*, accessed December 18, 2025, [https://www.accesstoinsight.org/tipitaka/sn/sn56/sn56.011.harv.html]

CHAPTER SEVEN — The Ending of the House

1. Bhikkhu Ñāṇamoli and Bhikkhu Bodhi, trans., *The Connected Discourses of the Buddha: A Translation of the Saṃyutta Nikāya*. (Boston: Wisdom Publications, 2000), SN 12.1–12.20
2. Bhikkhu Ñāṇamoli and Bhikkhu Bodhi, trans., *The Middle Length Discourses of the Buddha*, MN 36 (Mahāsaccaka Sutta).
3. Acharya Buddharakkhita, trans., *The Dhammapada: The Buddha's Path of Wisdom*. (Kandy: Buddhist Publication Society, 1985), verses 153–154.
4. Bhikkhu Bodhi, trans., *The Numerical Discourses of the Buddha*, AN 4.23; AN 6.44.
5. Bhikkhu Ñāṇamoli and Bhikkhu Bodhi, trans., *The Middle Length Discourses of the Buddha: A Translation of the Majjhima Nikāya* (Boston: Wisdom Publications, 1995), MN 36.
6. Bhikkhu Bodhi, trans., *The Connected Discourses of the Buddha: A Translation of the Saṃyutta Nikāya* (Boston: Wisdom Publications, 2000), SN 45.8.
7. Bhikkhu Ñāṇamoli and Bhikkhu Bodhi, trans., *The Middle Length Discourses of the Buddha: A Translation of the Majjhima Nikāya* (Boston: Wisdom Publications, 1995), MN 4.
8. Bhikkhu Bodhi, trans., *The Connected Discourses of the Buddha: A Translation of the Saṃyutta Nikāya* (Boston: Wisdom Publications, 2000), SN 12.51.
9. Buddhaghosa, *The Path of Purification (Visuddhimagga)*, trans. Bhikkhu Ñāṇamoli (Kandy: Buddhist Publication Society, 2010), XXII.76–78.
10. Acharya Buddharakkhita, trans., *The Dhammapada: The Buddha's Path of Wisdom* (Kandy: Buddhist Publication Society, 1985), vv. 153–154.
11. Bhikkhu Bodhi, trans., *The Connected Discourses of the Buddha: A Translation of the Saṃyutta Nikāya* (Boston: Wisdom Publications, 2000), SN 12.1–12.20.
12. Bhikkhu Bodhi, trans., *The Connected Discourses of the Buddha: A Translation of the Saṃyutta Nikāya* (Boston: Wisdom Publications, 2000), SN 22.59 (Anattalakkhaṇa Sutta).
13. Bhikkhu Ñāṇamoli and Bhikkhu Bodhi, trans., *The Middle Length Discourses of the Buddha: A Translation of the Majjhima Nikāya* (Boston: Wisdom Publications, 1995), MN 26.
14. Bhikkhu Bodhi, trans., *The Connected Discourses of the Buddha: A Translation of the Saṃyutta Nikāya* (Boston: Wisdom Publications, 2000), SN 22.59; see also MN 72.

CHAPTER EIGHT — The World as It Is Seen

1. Bhikkhu Bodhi, trans., *The Connected Discourses of the Buddha: A Translation of the Saṃyutta Nikāya* (Boston: Wisdom Publications, 2000), SN 22.95 (Phena Sutta).
2. Edward Conze, trans., *The Diamond Sutra and The Sutra of Hui-neng* (New York: Random House, 1959); Robert A. F. Thurman, trans., *The Holy Teaching of*

Notes

Vimalakīrti: A Mahāyāna Scripture (University Park: Pennsylvania State University Press, 1976).
3. Bhikkhu Bodhi, trans., *The Connected Discourses of the Buddha: A Translation of the Saṃyutta Nikāya* (Boston: Wisdom Publications, 2000), SN 22.22; SN 22.59.
4. Edward Conze, trans., *The Diamond Sutra and The Sutra of Hui-neng* (New York: Random House, 1959); Robert A. F. Thurman, trans., *The Holy Teaching of Vimalakīrti: A Mahāyāna Scripture* (University Park: Pennsylvania State University Press, 1976).
5. Bhikkhu Bodhi, trans., *The Connected Discourses of the Buddha: A Translation of the Saṃyutta Nikāya* (Boston: Wisdom Publications, 2000), SN 22.95 (Phena Sutta).
6. Ibid.
7. Bhikkhu Bodhi, *The Connected Discourses of the Buddha*, SN 22.82.
8. Ibid.
9. Edward Conze, trans., *The Diamond Sutra and The Sutra of Hui-neng* (New York: Random House, 1959); Robert A. F. Thurman, trans., *The Holy Teaching of Vimalakīrti: A Mahāyāna Scripture* (University Park: Pennsylvania State University Press, 1976).
10. Bhikkhu Bodhi, *The Connected Discourses of the Buddha*, SN 22.95.
11. Ibid.
12. Ibid.
13. Edward Conze, *The Diamond Sutra*, in *The Diamond Sutra and The Sutra of Hui-neng* (New York: Random House, 1959).

CHAPTER NINE — Nimitta, Visions, and the Shifting Texture of Consciousness

1. Bhikkhu Bodhi, trans., *The Numerical Discourses of the Buddha: A Translation of the Aṅguttara Nikāya* (Boston: Wisdom Publications, 2012), 108–9 (AN 1.51–52).
2. Bhikkhu Bodhi, *The Numerical Discourses of the Buddha*, AN 10.60.
3. Bhikkhu Bodhi, *The Numerical Discourses of the Buddha*, AN 5.28.
4. Bhikkhu Ñāṇamoli and Bhikkhu Bodhi, trans., *The Middle Length Discourses of the Buddha: A Translation of the Majjhima Nikāya* (Boston: Wisdom Publications, 1995), 938–43 (MN 118).
5. Bhikkhu Ñāṇamoli and Bhikkhu Bodhi, *The Middle Length Discourses of the Buddha*, MN 128.
6. Ibid.
7. Maurice Walshe, trans., *The Long Discourses of the Buddha: A Translation of the Dīgha Nikāya* (Boston: Wisdom Publications, 1995), 67–73 (DN 2).
8. Bhikkhu Ñāṇamoli and Bhikkhu Bodhi, trans., *The Middle Length Discourses of the Buddha: A Translation of the Majjhima Nikāya* (Boston: Wisdom Publications, 1995), MN 118.
9. Bhikkhu Bodhi, trans., *The Numerical Discourses of the Buddha: A Translation of the Aṅguttara Nikāya* (Boston: Wisdom Publications, 2012), AN 10.60.
10. Bhikkhu Ñāṇamoli and Bhikkhu Bodhi, trans., *The Middle Length Discourses of the Buddha: A Translation of the Majjhima Nikāya* (Boston: Wisdom Publications, 1995), MN 128.

11. Bhikkhu Bodhi, *The Numerical Discourses of the Buddha: A Translation of the Aṅguttara Nikāya*, AN 1.51–52.
12. Bhikkhu Ñāṇamoli and Bhikkhu Bodhi, *The Middle Length Discourses of the Buddha*, MN 128.
13. Ibid.
14. Bhikkhu Bodhi, trans., *The Connected Discourses of the Buddha: A Translation of the Saṃyutta Nikāya* (Boston: Wisdom Publications, 2000), SN 22.82.
15. Bhikkhu Bodhi, *The Connected Discourses of the Buddha: A Translation of the Saṃyutta Nikāya*, SN 22.95.

CHAPTER TEN — Dream Yoga Before Dream Yoga

1. Bhikkhu Ñāṇamoli and Bhikkhu Bodhi, trans., *The Middle Length Discourses of the Buddha: A Translation of the Majjhima Nikāya* (Boston: Wisdom Publications, 1995), Majjhima Nikāya 20.
2. Bhikkhu Bodhi, trans., *The Numerical Discourses of the Buddha: A Translation of the Aṅguttara Nikāya* (Boston: Wisdom Publications, 2012), Aṅguttara Nikāya 3.16.
3. Maurice Walshe, trans., *The Long Discourses of the Buddha: A Translation of the Dīgha Nikāya* (Boston: Wisdom Publications, 1995), Dīgha Nikāya 16.
4. Bhikkhu Bodhi, trans., *The Connected Discourses of the Buddha: A Translation of the Saṃyutta Nikāya* (Boston: Wisdom Publications, 2000), Saṃyutta Nikāya 47.40.
5. Bhikkhu Ñāṇamoli and Bhikkhu Bodhi, *The Middle Length Discourses of the Buddha*, MN 117–118.
6. Bhikkhu Bodhi, *The Numerical Discourses of the Buddha*, AN 3.16.
7. Bhikkhu Ñāṇamoli and Bhikkhu Bodhi, *The Middle Length Discourses of the Buddha*, MN 10.
8. Bhikkhu Bodhi, *The Connected Discourses of the Buddha*, SN 12.2.
9. Bhikkhu Ñāṇamoli and Bhikkhu Bodhi, *The Middle Length Discourses of the Buddha*, MN 10.

CHAPTER ELEVEN — The Quiet Before the Last Journey

1. Maurice Walshe, trans., *The Long Discourses of the Buddha: A Translation of the Dīgha Nikāya* (Boston: Wisdom Publications, 1995), 231–277, "Mahāparinibbāna Sutta" (DN 16).
2. Ibid.
3. Ibid.
4. Ibid.
5. Ibid.
6. Ibid.
7. Ibid.
8. Ibid.
9. Ibid.
10. Ibid.
11. Ibid.
12. Ibid.

Notes

13. Ibid.
14. Ibid.
15. Ibid.
16. Ibid.

CHAPTER TWELVE —
Dreaming in the Modern World

1. Bodhi, Bhikkhu, trans. *The Connected Discourses of the Buddha: A Translation of the Saṃyutta Nikāya*. Boston: Wisdom Publications, 2000. SN 12.44 (Lokasutta), 593–594 and SN 12.62, 605–606.

CONCLUSION: The Quiet
Where Dream and Dawn Meet

1. Bhikkhu Ñāṇamoli and Bhikkhu Bodhi, trans., *The Middle Length Discourses of the Buddha: A Translation of the Majjhima Nikāya* (Boston: Wisdom Publications, 1995), MN 1 (Mūlapariyāya Sutta) and MN 18 (Madhupiṇḍika Sutta).
2. Buddhaghosa, *The Path of Purification (Visuddhimagga)*, trans. Bhikkhu Ñāṇamoli (Kandy, Sri Lanka: Buddhist Publication Society, 2010), XII.55–57.
3. Bhikkhu Ñāṇamoli and Bhikkhu Bodhi, *The Middle Length Discourses of the Buddha: A Translation of the Majjhima Nikāya*, MN 109 and MN 111.

BIBLIOGRAPHY

Bays, Gwendolyn, trans. *The Lalitavistara Sūtra: The Voice of the Buddha*. 2 vols. Berkeley: Dharma Publishing, 1983.

Bodhi, Bhikkhu, trans. *The Connected Discourses of the Buddha: A Translation of the Saṃyutta Nikāya*. Boston: Wisdom Publications, 2000.

Bodhi, Bhikkhu, trans. *The Numerical Discourses of the Buddha: A Translation of the Aṅguttara Nikāya*. Boston: Wisdom Publications, 2012.

Buddhaghosa. *The Path of Purification (Visuddhimagga)*. Trans. Bhikkhu Ñāṇamoli. Kandy: Buddhist Publication Society, 2010.

Buddharakkhita, Acharya, trans. *The Dhammapada: The Buddha's Path of Wisdom*. Kandy: Buddhist Publication Society, 1985.

Conze, Edward, trans. *The Diamond Sutra and the Sutra of Hui-neng*. New York: Random House, 1959.

Cowell, E. B., ed. *The Jātaka or Stories of the Buddha's Former Births*. 6 vols. Cambridge: Cambridge University Press, 1895–1907.

Doniger, Wendy. *Dreams, Illusion, and Other Realities*. Chicago: University of Chicago Press, 1984.

Gethin, Rupert. *The Foundations of Buddhism*. Oxford: Oxford University Press, 1998.

Ñāṇamoli, Bhikkhu, and Bhikkhu Bodhi, trans. *The Middle Length Discourses of the Buddha: A Translation of the Majjhima Nikāya*. Boston: Wisdom Publications, 1995.

Nyanaponika Thera, trans. "Dhammacakkappavattana Sutta: Setting the Wheel of Dhamma in Motion (SN 56.11)." *Access to Insight*. Accessed December 18, 2025. https://www.accesstoinsight.org/tipitaka/sn/sn56/sn56.011.nysa.html.

Stickgold, Robert, and Matthew P. Walker. "Sleep-Dependent Memory Consolidation and Reconfiguration." *Journal of Sleep Research* 14, no. 3 (2005): 213–223. https://doi.org/10.1111/j.1365-2869.2005.00437.x.

Strong, John S. *The Buddha: A Short Biography*. Oxford: Oneworld, 2001.

Thanissaro Bhikkhu, trans. "Bhaya-bherava Sutta: Fear & Terror (MN 4)." *Access to Insight*. Accessed December 18, 2025. https://www.accesstoinsight.org/tipitaka/mn/mn.004.than.html.

Thurman, Robert A. F., trans. *The Holy Teaching of Vimalakīrti: A Mahāyāna Scripture*. University Park: Pennsylvania State University Press, 1976.

Walshe, Maurice, trans. *The Long Discourses of the Buddha: A Translation of the Dīgha Nikāya*. Boston: Wisdom Publications, 1995.

Young, Serenity. *Dreaming in the Lotus: Buddhist Dream Narrative, Imagery, and Practice*. Boston: Wisdom Publications, 1999.

www.ingramcontent.com/pod-product-compliance
Lightning Source LLC
Chambersburg PA
CBHW022015290426
44109CB00015B/1174